What respected No-Compromise Leaders are saying about

Wake Up!

"Wake Up! simply makes sense and brings to light the tough questions and the difficult situations all entrepreneurs face. Neil Ducoff has created something that will undoubtedly change people's lives, improve employee job satisfaction, and force leaders to look within themselves to find where they need to begin to fix their businesses!"

John T. Harms, founder and CEO, Millennium by Harms Software Inc.

"If you can't take the heat or don't want the truth, don't read this book! Neil Ducoff speaks the truth when he says almost all business problems are the result of executives compromising when they should stand up. This book is the antidote to weak, poor decisions!"

Jim Horan, president, The One Page Business Plan Company

"This book will make you smarter, happier, richer, more confident, prepared to make better decisions and the envy of your competitors. Read it before they do!"

Matthew Cross, president, LeadershipAlliance.com; author, *Get Your Priorities Straight*

"Simple, relevant and practical. Neil has stuffed *Wake Up!* with golden nuggets that everyone would love to read, be inspired and be a better 'no compromise,' innovative leader. *Wake Up!* is all about leadership innovations."

Praveen Gupta, director, Center for Innovation Science and Applications, Illinois Institute of Technology

"Ducoff does it again! *Wake Up!* is brilliant and to the point. His extensive leadership research and experience makes this a phenomenal source for any business."
John R. DiJulius III, author, *What's the Secret? To providing a world-class customer experience*

"I 'woke up' 18 months ago after reading Neil Ducoff's *No-Compromise Leadership*. My personal brand and identity needed an immediate overhaul. *NCL's* framework was my compass. Neil's weekly Monday Morning Wake-Ups sustained my journey. I was just promoted to vice president. Read *Wake Up!* today. Let it bring out the best in you and your company."
Robert Korpak, Vice President, Strategic Implementation, Webster Bank

"Neil Ducoff cuts through all the BS in the leadership genre and punches you squarely in the face with *Wake Up!*

You won't find mice moving cheese here; the author continues the theme of his first book, *No-Compromise Leadership,* by absolutely refusing to compromise on any of the core values and principles. The style is blunt and opinionated, backed by his own experience, wisdom and success.

If you're satisfied with the status quo, then validate your place in life with any number of the parable-laden placations on the market. If you're sick of lollipops and puppy dogs, and you're ready for a good kick in the pants, accept no compromise!"
Jim Bouchard, author, *Think Like a Blackbelt*

"In these economic times, we all need a Wake Up! Neil Ducoff's book delivers one powerful and insightful dose after another. I can personally attest to the success of utilizing Neil's "no-compromise leadership" systems. His books and business philosophies have been pivotal to my success and have allowed me to shape my destiny as a business leader."
Scott Sharrow, general manager, Arden Hills Resort, Sacramento, Calif.

"This is the perfect time for Neil's new book. As business leaders, we're facing more challenges (and opportunities) than ever before. *Wake Up!* offers important thinking on just about anything we face in our organizations. Open the book to any page and you'll find something relevant and impactful."

Dennis Snow, author; president, Snow & Associates, Inc.

"'It' is a very special thing in business. 'It' is a spot so sweet that you want to run out and tell everyone what it is like. Neil knows 'it' and shares it with you on every page. *Wake Up!* is one good book."

Jack Stack, CEO, SRC Holdings Corp; author, *The Great Game of Business*

"I have great respect for Neil's knowledge, focus, and passion. *Wake Up!* is another shining example of his never-ending quest to help individuals achieve next-level success by following his no-compromise leadership strategies."

Paula Kent Meehan, founder, Redken Laboratories; President, Kenquest

"Finally, a true business book for the short attention-span generation. Super-relevant, bite-sized business builders – or should I say business blasters. (They're that impactful!) Neil's wit is so pervasive and his insights are so right on that after I read every chapter, I felt as though I'd just had a conversation with him. This is a must-have resource for any successful business."

John Moroney, vice president of Education, Kao USA – Goldwell & KMS California

"In a competitive world where many people don't want to take responsibility, this is a great book about how to take responsibility and advance your career. Neil is a master at providing substantive insights along with examples on how to maximize your own potential."

Marc Kramer, executive director, The Private Investors Forum

"Neil's book is a compendium of reminders that compromise never sleeps. Retaining the integrity and appreciating the value of your brand (your most valuable asset) requires vigilance, guts, and a willingness to embrace and anticipate change, especially when it makes you least comfortable."
Mark O'Brien, principal, O'Brien Communications Group

"Neil Ducoff once again finds a way to light a fire under every leader beginning with the importance of the often underrated – but always necessary – act of just believing. In these pages, we are reminded without exception that the leader must take responsibility for the tone of every facet of the organization and chisel a masterpiece out of the block of granite that is the company. We must "do what others will not and push forward even (and especially) when we think we no longer can."
Mike Bosley, president, Beam's Seatbelts

"Reading Neil's first book propelled us to initiate actions, which had a profound impact on improving our business. For this I am forever grateful to Neil. His Monday Morning Wake-Up messages kept us going. This new book will motivate us to sustain the improvements we have already started because of his inspired teachings."
Catherine Brillantes-Turvill, president, Nurture Spa Village, Philippines

Also by Neil Ducoff

NO-COMPROMISE LEADERSHIP:
A Higher Standard of Leadership Thinking and Behavior

FAST FORWARD:
The Salon/Spa Industry's Definitive Business Management
Reference Guide for Owners, Managers and Key Staff

Wake Up!

Inspiring and challenging strategies
on what it takes to be a
No-Compromise Leader

By Neil Ducoff

CENTERBROOK • CONNECTICUT

Published by Strategies
40 Main Street, Suite 7
Centerbrook, Connecticut 06409
www.strategies.com

For orders other than individual consumers, Strategies grants discounts on purchases of 10 or more copies of single titles for bulk use, special markets or premium use. For further details, contact:
Strategies
40 Main Street, Suite 7, Centerbrook, CT 06409
tel (800) 417-4848

Edited by Mara Dresner
Book design by Cameron C. Taylor
Cover illustration by John Woodcock/istockphoto.com
Book set in Minion Pro and Myriad Pro

Library of Congress Control Number: 2012932173
Ducoff, Neil.
   WAKE UP! : Inspiring and challenging strategies on what it takes
   to be a No-Compromise Leader / Neil Ducoff. – 1st ed.
      270p. | 22.4cm.
   ISBN 9780984862009
   1. Business Management.   2. Leadership.   3. Entrepreneurship.
   4. Creative Thinking.   I. Title.

First Strategies Press Edition
10 9 8 7 6 5 4 3 2
Printed in the United States of America

Dedication

This book is dedicated to my amazing team at Strategies.
Every one of you believes in the Strategies dream.
You help me do what I cannot do alone.

Wish you could have held this book.
Ron Ducoff
1947 – 2012

Acknowledgements

My sincere gratitude to Jayne Morehouse who encouraged me to create my Monday Morning Wake-Up series. You would not be holding *Wake Up!* in your hands had it not been for Jayne.

No one knows me as a writer better than my long-time and trusted editor, Mara Dresner. An accomplished writer in her own right, Mara continues to coach and inspire me to connect with that special inner place to refine and perfect my writer's voice that communicates my thoughts and ideas to the world through words. Thank you, Mara, for not only for the tireless hours, weeks and months of editing *Wake Up!*, but for continuously raising the bar to make me a better writer. You are truly a no-compromise editor.

It takes a special creative talent to transform hundreds of pages of words into a book that is visually appealing and a pleasure to read. That creative talent is my graphic designer of many years, Cameron Taylor. Thank you for designing the perfect cover for *Wake Up!* and for your expert attention to every page, every pull quote and every graphic element. Cameron, you played a key role in the creation of a very special book, which will inspire readers for years to come.

A very heartfelt thank you to my team at Strategies Corporate Offices and to every Strategies Coach. You're the ones who live with and share the no-compromise leadership mantra every day. You give inspiration and meaning to my work in ways that only true believers can. Together, we help leaders discover a better way to do business. Together, we show leaders how to build authentic no-compromise cultures, leading them to the true path to excellence and extraordinary success.

Lastly, I want to acknowledge all of the business leaders who trust and look to Strategies to find a better way, for allowing us into your companies and for attending our seminars. The stories in *Wake Up!* were inspired by you to help you. That's the secret sauce that makes every Monday Morning Wake-Up resonate with readers at the core of their leadership thinking where profound change begins.

Table of Contents

Chapter 5 :: Culture

Chapter 6 :: Future

Chapter 7 :: You

Chapter 8 :: Strategies

Foreword

When Neil Ducoff writes, I read. I ponder. I reflect. It's not just that he has an important message (although he does). For the past several years, I have been the first set of eyes on Neil's work.

Editing comes with a sacred responsibility. The goal is ever to ensure that the reader is enlightened, challenged and inspired. The editor works to make certain that message is most effectively received, while maintaining the integrity of the work and the voice of the writer.

Neil's voice is clear and unwavering. In the years we've worked together, I've seen his voice strengthen, as he has amassed an influential body of work. He's not afraid to confront the reader, the leader, with a powerful message and sometimes, a punch to the gut.

He takes on the issues that seldom get discussed in the lengthy canon of business topics: the blockages, inconsistencies, fears and lack of accountability that hold leaders back from having the companies they desire.

Neil understands that it is in these gray issues that entrepreneurial careers are made or broken. As a business owner, educator and coach, he has seen the vast mix of skills, personality and ambition that comprise one's leadership style and shapes companies across the globe.

If Neil is writing about it, it matters. His Monday Morning Wake-Up column has become a must-read for thousands of leaders who strive to grow and take their companies further, without excuse.

When these concise columns arrive to my inbox, I feel a bit like Forrest Gump – I never know exactly what I'm going to get. Some columns, we've discussed at length and the column reflects our conversation. Other times, we've discussed an issue at length and Neil then writes on a totally different topic. Still others are a complete surprise to me, frequently keying off a recent class or client experience.

While it's not exactly opening a present on Christmas morning, there is still a feeling of anticipation. I am seldom disappointed.

Leaders – human as they are – are subject to numerous foibles and are continually a work-in-progress. Neil strives to spur leaders to ever-improving levels of communication, accountability, profitable growth – what is needed to succeed in boon times and down economies.

We call this collection the best-of-the-best, although that might be a misnomer. It is more precisely a better-than-the-best compendium. We worked to truly make *Wake Up!* a timeless resource. That meant not using some columns that were impactful when they were first written but have become a bit out-of-date. Other columns got new introductions; some were combined and rewritten to use the strongest messages from each. *Wake Up!* is more than a cup of Joe – it is an in-your-face double shot of espresso.

This is not the type of book that you'll read start to finish like a tense crime novel. You'll pick and choose what columns speak to you in any given moment. Don't worry about reading the chapters in order. This is a case where it's most assuredly "all good."

At times you may meet a topic with resistance and defense. You may be spurred to action – or just anger. Or, you may read several chapters in a row, thinking, "Yes, yes, yes," and then not put thought into practice.

That's what this book is here for – to meet you on your leadership path and to illuminate the road ahead. You may not want to hear what's being said; you may not be ready to hear it. Read it anyway. Walk away, and then reread it. The columns that make you the most uncomfortable are most likely the ones you need the most. Have your management team and staff read them. Discuss them and come up with an action plan for your business.

Neil writes about the business challenges that lie in the shadows. He's brave enough to shine a light on the areas that many would prefer to leave alone. He's not afraid to stir the pot. The question is, "Are you ready?"

This book offers guidance, insight and inspiration that you won't find anywhere else. What you do with it is up to you.

No compromise!

Mara Dresner
Vice President of Communications
Strategies

Preface

I've been writing about business and leadership for more than four decades. After countless articles, special reports, training materials, a business resource book and an award-winning leadership book, I'm still amazed where the all the words, thoughts and ideas come from. My high-school English teacher would likely proclaim the volume of my work a miracle. I simply regard my writing as a gift that has allowed me to help leaders and companies find their way through an increasingly complex world.

The idea for the Monday Morning Wake-Up (MMWU) started forming in late 2007. I was looking for a way to deliver something of value to my company's impressive list of e-mail followers. I wanted to create something readers would look forward to every week, something that would challenge them to stretch and grow as leaders. With my No-Compromise Leadership book scheduled for publication in 2008, I wanted each installment to build on the no-compromise leadership concept. And what better way to start the week than with a powerful leadership message?

The concept of the MMWU was simple. Each weekly installment would be short, compelling and hit a key topic or issue that's on the minds of business owners and leaders. I would give each one an extra-special kick with my no-compromise leadership thinking and behavior. We'd send it out free of charge, sprinkle it with a few promos for Strategies' seminars, coaching and other services – and pray that it goes viral.

MMWU blasts off

So, just after 6 a.m. Eastern Time on January 21, 2008, the very first Monday Morning Wake-Up blasted into cyberspace.

As a speaker and a writer, I always have been eternally grateful for my ability to tap into the thinking of leaders and connect that thinking to critical business issues and concepts. I'm not talking soft connections; I'm talking about tapping into deep-rooted emotions, obstacles and anxiety that virtually every leader experiences in a quest to build a company. I know that I hit the mark as a speaker when I receive feedback that sounds like, "This is the information that I came here for." The more comments I receive as a writer, the more affirmation I have that my words are not only resonating – they're delivering implementable strategies.

Every MMWU concludes with a link to our WordPress blog for readers to post comments. And the comments instantly began hitting the blog. Immediate feedback is so amazing; it is an indicator of my effectiveness barometer in addressing the critical issues that leaders encounter every day.

I read every comment. I feed on your feedback. If a MMWU receives light response, I question why. Did I select a timely topic? Did I deliver sufficient insight? Were the solutions viable and detailed enough? Did I totally miss the mark? I hate when I feel as though I've missed the mark. I hate to waste my readers' time because the topic I selected didn't resonate. Yes, I take it personally. It keeps me pushing forward to deliver the best leadership strategies possible in a fast-read format.

When a MMWU inspires readers to post comments, they are without exception heartfelt remarks, personal stories of courage to overcome the challenges of leading, surviving and growing a company in today's fiercely predatory economy. Many are just appreciative notes. I internalize and process every comment. Why? Because your comments make me a better writer, speaker, consultant, coach and leadership mentor by honing my ability to address what matters; to deliver clarity and a compass to follow in these times of mass uncertainty.

Where MMWU topics are born

OK, I admit that I write most MMWUs on the preceding Friday. I typically get up before dawn to write them because I enjoy the solitude and serenity of a new day. It inspires me more than any other time of day. I also admit that the pressure of a drop-dead deadline is inspiration. My editor, Mara Dresner, is waiting for a fresh MMWU to arrive. My graphic designer, Cameron Taylor, is waiting for the edited version, so he can search for and select an appropriate image. Cameron is awesome at finding images that speak to the topic – often with a sense of humor. We hope you enjoy them.

I can't write a MMWU if it doesn't inspire me first. I seek out topics that delve deep into the nooks and crannies of leadership thinking and behavior. I look for topics that challenge leaders. I want my readers to think, "How did Neil know I was stuck on that?" If there is any one theme to my MMWUs, it's to get leaders to accept and take ownership in the outcomes they enabled. To stop their culture-destroying process of "blame, justify and defend." That is the essence of each MMWU – to lead above the trivialities that bog leaders down in all that stuff that destroys companies from within.

Pride and passion

More than anything I've ever written, this collection of MMWUs represents the best practices that every leader needs to permanently embed his or her thinking and behaviors. *Wake Up!* is a practical guide to what it takes to be a no-compromise leader. Not a dictatorial and inflexible leader, rather a leader who inspires excellence and the collective achievement of the extraordinary. *Wake Up!* is about doing the work of leadership. It's about getting to that elusive next level rather than giving it lip service. It's about taking ownership in what's right and wrong with your company. It's about solutions and boldly taking those steps into the amazing places that await all no-compromise leaders.

Lastly, *Wake Up!* is about the rewards that exceed the monetary. It's about building business cultures capable of busting through barriers that stall other companies. It's about innovating new business realities that can only be described as world class.

Wake Up! is collection of strategies to take you and your company to remarkable places. It's a book to be used – not just read. It's a roadmap to your wildest dreams.

Use it.

No compromise.

Neil Ducoff
Founder & CEO
Strategies

Sign up for MMWU! at www.strategies.com.

Neilism:
Most leaders talk a better game
than they play.

CHAPTER

1

Finding
Your "It"

Believe

There is extraordinary power in the simple act of believing. In and of itself, believing is the process of weighing the pros and cons, and all the possible outcomes, to draw a conclusion of what is and what can be. Believing is not an absolute but rather a state of mind. It's your perception of who you are and the world around you. Believing serves as your internal compass.

As a leader, what you believe, and how completely you believe, is critical to establishing the accuracy of your internal compass. Believe a little and your compass will waiver. Believe a lot and your compass will guide you to the desired outcome. When you don't believe at all, your compass is useless – and you are lost.

- **You first:** As a leader, you must believe in yourself before others can believe in you. No one is going to be inspired by a leader lacking self-confidence and the determination to win. When you believe in yourself – even in the toughest of situations – others will believe in you. It's in those difficult times that you most need to believe in yourself. How you lead in tough times defines you as a no-compromise leader.

- **Reset your compass:** Time and time again I see leaders blaming staff for lackluster performance, missing goals and costly mistakes. Most often, the cure is as simple as resetting the leader's compass. People, teams and organizations rise to the challenge for causes they believe in. When work is all about the numbers and hitting goals, the emotion and passion for winning is in short supply. Resetting your compass means reconnecting with the vision and purpose of the company and understanding that numbers and hitting goals are simply measurements of what you and your team believe in.

- **Believing you can win doesn't mean you will win:** "I/we can't do it" thinking does not inspire great achievements and extraordinary performance. Believing in the possibility of winning – of achieving breakthroughs – is what carries you and those you lead over the rough patches. Not getting the win after putting up a good fight still carries a lot of fulfillment. And there's so much to learn from almost winning. Just a few tweaks may be all that's required to cross the finish line. It's pure agony to play any business game believing that you're going to lose.

- **Live it first:** We all have our moments of doubt. There may be times when we question if we're good enough, smart enough or tenacious enough. But believing in yourself, your team and your company is where amazing journeys begin. Step back from the daily craziness and reconnect with what you believe in about yourself, your team and your company. When you live what you believe, others will follow you on your journey.

- **Celebrate the imperfections:** I have to throw this thought into the mix. It's the imperfections that make us unique, that make our companies unique. There are things about me that are imperfect. Just like all the things I naturally do well and exceed at, there are things I goof up. It all makes me who I am. And that often gives others and me stuff to laugh about. Yet, I never allow the imperfections to compromise what I believe in. That perhaps is the most important thought to remember. ✒

When you live what you believe, **others will follow you** on your journey.

Your passion will see you through

There is a dividing line that separates leaders from no-compromise leaders. On one side, "leader" is something that describes a title or job. It's simply the work you do. On the other side of the dividing line is an inherent and unmistakable emotional intensity radiating from the no-compromise leader. It's like a gravitational pull to a higher calling that converges on the vision and greater purpose of the company. It's intense passion; and it's impossible to be a no-compromise leader without it. Why? If you don't have passion for what you do, it's just too easy to give up – to compromise. The no-compromise leader says, "We're going to make the world a better place for all," and believes this with every fiber of his or her being.

Passion fuels a higher calling and a natural enthusiasm to all that you do. So much so that others can sense and capture that same passion. The no-compromise leader's passion attracts and engages others in the most positive way. That shared passion then lifts the performance of the entire company. Consider any great leader in history, business or otherwise, and you will find an innate passion as the driving force behind his or her accomplishments.

- **What will your company look like in five years?** These are crazy and tense times for all leaders. To avoid getting consumed and dragged down by today's challenges and bad economic news, raise your sights and target what you want your company to look like in five years. Paint a bold picture of success and opportunity. Make it so cool and enticing that you'll want to lead your team there.

- **What does your company flag look like?** Yes, I said, "flag." If you're going to lead your team to victory, you'll need a flag. Assemble a "flag design team" and charge them with the mission of creating a flag that your company will carry through this recession to that cool place you defined in your vision. There's no better way to lift the spirits of your team than getting them fired up for a journey back to good times.

- **Flip your switch from reactive to proactive:** It's hard to keep your passion for business and leadership burning bright when you're stuck reacting to situations. Going proactive puts you on the offensive. Going proactive lifts you up so you can lift your team up. Going proactive means innovative new strategies and 100% execution.

If you have the fire in your gut to achieve your dreams against all odds, you have passion. If you get excited and light up when you tell others about your work, you have passion. When you hear your employees talking about their work and the company with the same passion as you – your passion for success has created a company-wide mojo that's virtually unstoppable. 🦃

When employees talk
about the company
with the same passion as you,
you created a
company-wide mojo
that's virtually
unstoppable.

Your business model: facelift or overhaul?

I once wrote a column that stated, "The economy has created a new reality that requires your business model to adapt at a faster pace: The moment you think you have your business model just right – start questioning it and exploring what needs to change. … If you and your company are resistant to change today, your business model is already behind the curve." On my blog, I received a number of comments asking me to explain my statement in more detail.

About 12 years ago a mentor of mine suggested that I consider publishing a version of *Strategies* magazine for travel agencies and agents. Initially it sounded like a good fit; mostly entrepreneurial businesses in need of business guidance and advice. There was only one issue to consider – how was the Internet going to impact the travel agent industry? At the time, Expedia and Travelocity were just ramping up. After some consideration, I told my mentor that the title of the first issue would be, "The Internet: Kiss your ass goodbye." The travel agency business model crumbled as consumers and business travelers began booking travel online.

Blockbuster's business model was based on "brick and mortar" locations for video rentals. Netflix took an entirely different approach with a web-based monthly subscription that mailed selected DVDs to your mailbox. The two business models competed head to head until Netflix shifted its business model to streaming on-demand video selections. I stopped going to our local Blockbuster when Apple TV was released. Now, Netflix, Hulu and the new kid on the block, the Roku, are bringing the convenience of streaming video of a massive array of affordable on-demand content to your TV. Blockbuster hesitated to change its business model and is now fighting for survival to catch up while closing stores en masse.

Newspapers and magazines are shifting their business models away from print. Book publishers, spurred on by the success of Amazon's Kindle, are shifting to digital downloads. Analysts predict that digital book sales will increase 68% in 2011. Meanwhile, the brick-and-mortar Barnes

& Nobles of the world are fighting the same catch-up game as Blockbuster by introducing their own digital book readers.

Over the past two decades, salons have been jumping on the spa bandwagon business model. In the process, gift-card revenue became a vital cash flow. Then along came the economic downturn hitting a U.S. spa market that was already saturated. Add stretched-out hair appointments and more reserved consumer spending on gift cards, and expansion efforts that would have proved fruitful in good times, put enormous strain on cash flow today. I'm not suggesting that salons get out of the spa market or that spa-only establishments should open salons. My message is to brutally question your business model and isolate what's working and what's not. Go "no compromise" on your customer-service standards and practices. Maybe getting smaller today is the key to getting bigger tomorrow. Raise the bar higher. The worst thing to do is assume that you can't change your business model. You can. Every business can.

> If you and your company are **resistant to change today,** your business model is already behind the curve.

It doesn't matter if you own a medical practice, dry cleaning business, retail store or if you manufacture automobiles, every business model must adapt and be reinvented in order to survive. And here's the kicker – the viable lifespan of a business model is shrinking faster than anyone realizes.

So, does your business model need a facelift or an overhaul? Those are the only two choices you have. Well, there is a third and that's to do nothing 🐓

Getting off the hamster wheel

When leaders are stuck on the hamster wheel, they are essentially running at high speed, burning lots of energy and getting nowhere fast. It's being stuck in that daily rut of driving revenues, fighting cash flow, motivating unmotivated employees and trying to push projects across the finish line. It's working harder and gaining little, if any, ground. It's when that voice in your head keeps asking, "How long can you keep going like this?"

Fact: Getting off the hamster wheel is not easy. By the time you realize you're on it, you're already spinning so fast that jumping off seems outright dangerous. And if you slow down, all the fears, concerns and what-ifs may catch up to you. Well, here's another fact to chew on: Spinning on the hamster wheel is exhausting and unsustainable. You found a way to get on it, and now it's time to get off and regain control of your life and your company. The good news is that being stuck on the hamster wheel is one dilemma you can find a solution for.

- **STEP ONE – It's nothing more than a routine:** The first step to getting off the hamster wheel is to recognize it for what it is. It's a routine and a pattern of behavior that you can absolutely change – if you want to. Consider what happens when you go on vacation, take a long weekend, or attend a seminar or conference. You're forcing yourself into a new pattern of behavior that gives you a mental and physical break from spinning on the hamster wheel. Once you acknowledge that it's a routine you're stuck in – and that you have control over that routine – you can move to the next step.

- **STEP TWO – Something worth chasing:** Since you're getting nowhere on the hamster wheel, Step Two is about setting your sights on a set of goals that will inspire you to break out of your routine. You control your destiny. Too many leaders lose sight of this and allow situations to shape their behaviors. So, if you want to channel your time and energy on work that fulfills and excites, define exactly what that work is. Write it down. Immerse yourself in thoughts of actually doing that work every day. Call it manifesting or whatever you want – if you can't see it in your mind and feel it inside you, it's not real.

- **STEP THREE – Eliminate the blockages:** Just about every case of getting stuck on the hamster wheel involves a leadership blockage. I define a leadership blockage as tasks, responsibilities and decisions that you avoid like the plague. So much so that spinning on the hamster wheel feels like a better alternative than busting through your blockages. Getting off the hamster wheel means addressing all that stuff you've been avoiding. Dig into your financials and find that elephant that's been sucking the financial life out of your company and make a decision that will fix it. Stop running your company like a country club by putting in the structure, systems and accountability that define all great companies. Whatever your blockages are, now is the time to bust through them and reclaim control.

Getting off the hamster wheel is not easy.
By the time you realize you're on it,
you're already spinning so fast
that jumping off seems outright dangerous.

- **STEP FOUR – The risk is worth it:** I loathe the hamster wheel. Therefore, I design my work routine to avoid getting stuck. I have my work in the office where I write, create, lead and deal with stuff. (Yeah, I goof off a bit too. Goofing off balances the stress.) I also travel a lot for speaking and consulting. I design my work in ways to keep it engaging and fulfilling, so just when I feel like I'm getting stuck in a routine, I'm on to a new project. No, it isn't perfect, but it works for me. The key is taking the risk to step out of your comfort zone. To challenge yourself and continually raise your own success bar up a few rungs to make you stretch. Fact: Status quo is the hamster wheel.

- **STEP FIVE – Time and timing:** It took time for your routine to turn into a hamster wheel. It's going to take time to change your routine and replace it with one that's not only new and improved, one that will have you fall in love with your work and your company all over again. Only you can decide when you've had enough of getting nowhere on the hamster wheel. Only you can decide when it's time to take the risk of stepping off and busting through your blockages. Only you can define what goals and objectives are worth chasing. And only you can define what kind of work fulfills you. This all takes time.

In Chapter 8 of my *No-Compromise Leadership* book, there is an 18-month timeline for a culture shift. The same holds true for a personal culture shift. The first 30 days are critical. Making it through the first 90 days is essential. Push through the first six months and you have the best chance of busting free of the hamster wheel and taking your company to that elusive next level. No compromise. 🐦

Call it manifesting or whatever you want – **if you can't see it in your mind** and feel it inside you, it's not real.

How do I get off this thing?

It's time to stretch and fly high

I often talk about company culture shifts. If you strip away all the business jargon, culture shifts are nothing more than an upgrading of a company's behaviors. It's quite natural for behaviors to settle in after an upgrade. And that's exactly the problem with culture shifts. As the leader, you inspire, train, mentor and push your team up to that coveted next level. Getting there is the goal – that's what everyone is focused on. As new behaviors become the norm, the culture shift winds down. The goal has now become the accomplishment. But then what? It starts all over again because maintaining status quo leaves your company vulnerable to competitors that are aggressively pushing forward.

So let's change the scenario and bring this conversation to the face you see in the mirror. Consider the times in your life when you acknowledged that your personal behaviors needed an upgrade. Chances are that you felt unchallenged, stuck, frustrated, ineffective or just plain bored. You decide it's time for your very own culture shift – that it's time to stretch and push yourself to reach what you know is your full potential.

Personal culture shifts ramp up over time until bam! Enough is enough and you start plotting a new course for yourself. Call it an awakening, an epiphany or just you kicking your own butt – you finally lift your attention out of the quagmire of stuff you deal with every day and find yourself invigorated by new possibilities. What you're actually experiencing are the first stages of stretching your mind and imagination; you're getting your blood flowing to areas of thinking and behavior that fell dormant.

Do I have your attention? Do you feel like stretching? I bet you do, and that's awesome. However, there is a danger to stretching and having that transformational "bam" go off in your head. Your initial attempts at stretching and shifting to new behaviors will instantly be under attack by your current and deeply embedded behaviors and situation. That empowering "bam" can go "poof" in a blink. The key is to shift smoothly from the initial lift of stretching into a personal commitment, and then, total engagement.

As a business trainer, consultant and coach, it is a joy to see leaders experience the "bam" when they realize that it is often their own behaviors that were the root cause of their frustrations and feeling stuck. It's an even bigger epiphany when leaders realize that they need to change first, in order for their company to shift its culture. But just like diets and workout programs that begin with vigor, most sputter and die in a matter of days or weeks.

It's a joy to see leaders experience the "bam" when they realize that it is often their own behaviors that were the root cause of their **frustrations and feeling stuck.**

It's interesting how often we receive calls from leaders seeking coaching and training just after experiencing their "bam" moment and decision to stretch. After receiving insight into their issues and goals, we offer an overview of the work to be done. It's not unusual to hear a leader say, "We worked with coaches before and nothing changed." That statement gets my neck hairs on end because the one constant in all the failed efforts was the leader who complained he didn't get his money's worth. In such cases, it's the leader who wants big changes in the company's behavior to occur – but could not or would not change their behaviors. They want everything and everyone else to change but them.

The lesson here is that we as leaders must keep challenging ourselves to get better first, before we place that mandate on the backs of our employees. We not only need to keep stretching, we need to back that up with commitment and engagement. It's that simple and that complicated.

Delivering the no-compromise personal touch

A Chicago-area retailer is committed to delivering that special personal touch to customers. Susan Opeka is the owner of The Present Moment, which offers merchandise and programs to inspire the "heart, mind and soul." Opeka has focused on making her store a place where customers can come for a cup of coffee, a cookie and a break from all the bad news on television and in the papers.

At a time when a lot of customers seem to be holding back and wondering what the financial crisis means for them, savvy business players are on the offensive and rethinking new ways compete and thrive through tough times. And when the strategy is targeting the heart of the customer-service experience, it can be just what businesses need to create crucial lift in their companies. What's even more enticing about this strategy is that it costs little to implement.

If you're thinking, "We already do the personal touch thing," think again. If you and every employee in your business were given the ultimatum to deliver true and authentic no-compromise personal-touch experiences or lose every customer to a competitor, how much better would everyone perform? What level of personal touch would your clients experience? Describe it. Define it. Systematize it. Then, hold everyone accountable for delivering it all day, every day.

Indifference is the nemesis of customer service. That's right, indifference; that attitude clients encounter from employees who take their needs, time, money and loyalty for granted. Indifference may be present a lot or a little, but it's a sure bet that it's lurking somewhere in your business – and you need to find it and fix it fast.

Delivering the no-compromise personal touch to every client is a game changer. It ups the ante and channels your team's energy around the single most important asset your business has, your clients. It turns a visit to your company into something significantly more special and meaningful. It "serves" clients in the most nurturing ways possible by anticipating their needs and delivering the unexpected.

I know I'm preaching the obvious there. I also know you can do better – a lot better – delivering the personal touch if only you and your team take it on with no compromise as your one and only standard.

If delivering the no-compromise personal touch to your clients is just one puzzle piece to making it through these tough times unscathed, go for it. If it generates just $1 more in sales, go for it. If it puts a smile on a client's face, no compromise says, "If it needs to be done, get it done." 🐾

Indifference
is the nemesis of customer service.

When leaders have epiphanies

Ta da! In a gush of mental processing, you figured out the puzzle pieces and achieved a breakthrough of extraordinary, life-altering magnitude. Not only has your epiphany enlightened you, it has illuminated the path before you. You are in a different place where you see everything clearly. I witness leaders having epiphanies all the time. Heck, it's my job to guide leaders to have those epiphanies.

The good news is that when leaders have epiphanies, they are massively empowering and ignite a sense of urgency to innovate, to do things differently and to just get the change train out of the station. The bad news about leaders having epiphanies is that people around them often don't have a clue what's going on or where that train is going. How could they, with the leader up front in the engine, flailing his engineer hat around, shouting "woo hoo," and pushing the throttle to full speed ahead?

- **Beam me back, Scotty:** Epiphanies instantly transport leaders to a different place while leaving your team in the dust. Until you share your epiphany Kool-Aid with your team, they will perceive you and your epiphany as something from outer space. Until you invest the time to thoroughly download the why and wherefore of your epiphany to your team, your enlightenment or idea will frustrate those you lead instead of inspiring them.

- **Epiphanies signal change:** Not everyone is comfortable riding the change train. Some even refuse to get onboard. That's why it's essential that you balance your newfound enlightenment with determination and heavy doses of information. If your epiphany came with a user's guide, what would that look like? If your epiphany caused a shift in your leadership style or focus, it would sure help your employees figure out the new you if they could read about the updated features and how to use them. The same goes for any new system, business model or innovation.

- **Lead through the epiphany:** Don't push - lead. Epiphanies can be inspiring. In a Strategies "Beyond Being the Boss seminar," I did a segment on how to take a sabbatical for a month or so. Most initially balked at the idea saying, "There's no way I can take that much time off." After further exploration, ta da! The epiphanies went off like popcorn popping. Two leaders went back to their companies and announced their sabbaticals, focusing on the unique opportunity it presented to their team leaders and staff to prove themselves.

- **It's a seed - not a tree:** When epiphanies occur, they're in a fairly raw form. You may see the destination or outcome quite clearly, but the process or plan to get there only exists in the abstract. Epiphanies need time to bake, to gain texture and definition. Think of an epiphany as only giving you the first 15% of the solution. New thinking and behavior take time to lock in. Ideas or systems need to be tested. Sense of urgency is fine, but making a mad dash across a potential minefield can get you, and those who believe in you, blown up.

Think of an epiphany as only **giving you the first 15%** of the solution.

- **Epiphany or brain fart:** This is a tricky one to explain. Some epiphanies can be acts of desperation. I've seen leaders make some pretty bad decisions that only made matters worse. An epiphany can be a great idea but impractical to initiate at the time. And there are epiphanies that are just brain farts that you hope nobody notices. You feel it when a true epiphany occurs. An epiphany lights you up and energizes you. Even then, you need to see if the epiphany has staying power.

So, let your epiphanies materialize. Just manage them so they don't get out of control. 🐓

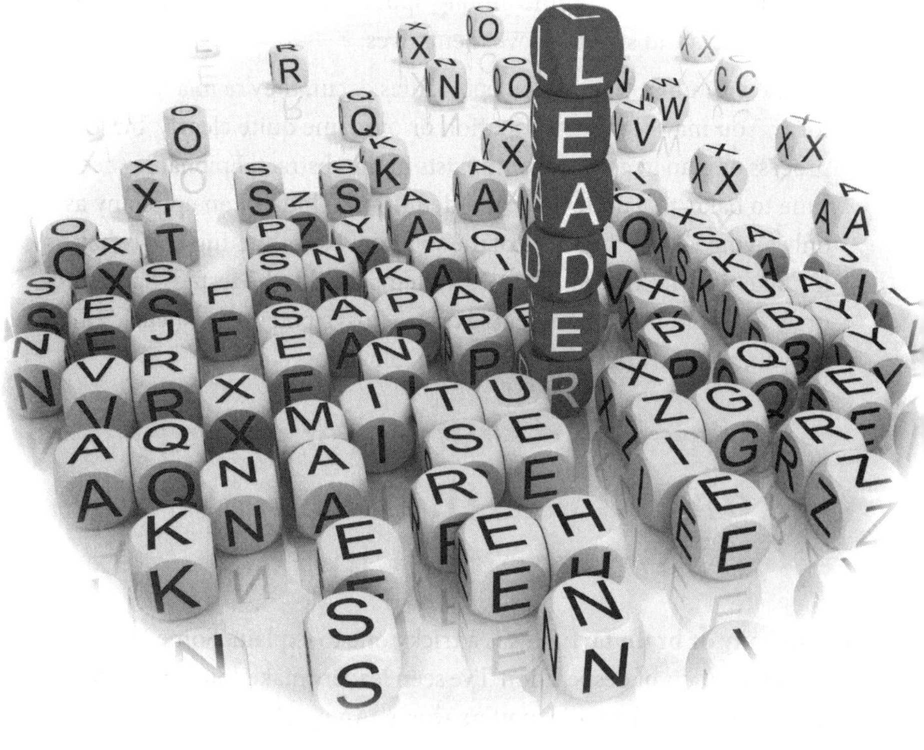
LEADER

Neilism:
We persevere. We overcome.
We are leaders.

Leadership

These days, it's great to be a leader

What a great time it is to be a leader. The economy is in flux. Money and cash flow is on everyone's mind. Employees are nervous. Customers are cautious, delaying purchases and looking for better deals. And, you've probably made some of your toughest leadership decisions in years. So why is this a great time to be a leader? The answer is extraordinarily simple – you are in control of your own destiny.

In these unprecedented and uncertain economic times, I cherish, respect and thrive in my role as the leader of my own company. I find solace knowing that my business experience, innovativeness, ability to identify and react to real and potential hazards, allows me to guide my company through tough times. I'm energized by the trust and support of my team. I am a leader, and I wouldn't trade my job or my responsibilities for anything.

Yes, we leaders must deal with stress and make decisions that thrust us out of our comfort zones. We can feel overwhelmed and overloaded. At times we may even feel unprepared, insecure and fearful. But as leaders, we know it's all part of the job. We persevere. We overcome. We are leaders.

Here are some simple reminders why it's great to be a leader:

- **If it is to be, it's up to me:** That's the essence of leadership. We control our own destinies. We can take our companies to any goal we set our minds on. We wait for no one. We can seize the moment. What greater freedom, growth and success could you ask for?

- **You have followers who trust and believe in you:** What an honor and privilege it is to be a leader – to have loyal followers who believe in and work to achieve a vision that's your creation. What more could you ask for?

- **You inspire others to reach their full potential:** As a leader, you help others achieve their dreams. You bring out the best in people. You take people to levels of success that even they didn't realize they could achieve. You make the lives of those around you better. What more could you ask for?

- **Today is your time to be your best:** Good times can cause leaders to get off their game and become content and lazy. Uncertain times bring out the best in leaders. Uncertain times challenge you to prove that you've got the right stuff. It's your opportunity to fix what's wrong in your business. It's your opportunity to innovate and lift your company to that next level you always talk about. What more could you ask for? 🐦

At times we may even
**feel unprepared, insecure
and fearful.**
But as leaders, we know
it's all part of the job.

What going 'no compromise' really means

Going no compromise will no doubt be the most significant personal change a leader makes in his or her leadership thinking and behavior. No compromise requires a leader to break through all of the emotional blockages that impede personal and business growth. It establishes the highest standards of performance and execution supported by a solid foundation of integrity and trust. Procrastination and blame are replaced with a sense of urgency and accountability. By design, no compromise turns problems and obstacles into innovative solutions and growth opportunities.

- **I will get it done:** Procrastinating is pure compromise. If you're committed to going no compromise, you're committing to getting things done. No compromise.

- **I will be accountable:** Accountability is the essence of trust. Delivering results, fulfilling commitments and demonstrating, through your actions and deeds, that you can be counted on by those you serve and lead. No compromise.

- **I will not avoid the tough stuff:** Sooner or later, every business encounters rough waters. As leader, you must engage and make the tough decisions that ensure the integrity of the company you lead. No compromise.

- **I will not be dictatorial and inflexible:** Going no compromise means leading with purpose and compassion – not heavy-handed tactics. Lead with passion and resolve. No compromise.

- **I will nurture and protect my company's culture:** The ultimate responsibility of the no-compromise leader is to create, maintain and protect the company's culture. It's the culture that attracts and keeps the best talent. It's the culture that builds customer loyalty. No compromise.

Strive to live these five bullet points and you will see a transformation not only in yourself, but in the company you lead. Just remember, once you commit to them, no compromise means there's no going back. 🐓

The ultimate responsibility
of the no-compromise leader
is to create, maintain
and protect
the company's culture.

Living No-Compromise Leadership

I remember the joy I felt the first time I held a printed copy of my book *No-Compromise Leadership: A Higher Standard of Leadership Thinking and Behavior.* Since then, the real reward is how the book and the concept of no-compromise leadership are changing the lives of leaders and their companies. Here are some of the comments that readers have shared:

- **"You wrote Part One about me."** I simply wrote about the common "compromises" that leaders make every day and how those compromises degrade and chip away their company culture. Procrastination, double standards and leadership blockages, such as confusing challenging conversations with confrontation. It was interesting how many leaders saw themselves in the examples and stories.

- **"It's hard work."** That's what leaders engaged in the process say about making the shift to no-compromise leadership. Yes, it is hard work – but it's doing the work of leadership and avoiding the easier and mediocre path of compromise. One reader told me how going no compromise was the toughest personal behavioral change he'd ever made. He's grown as a leader and his company's performance shows impressive and measurable results. Hard work and leadership are inseparable.

- **"The Four Business Outcomes gave me focus."** Productivity, profitability, staff retention and customer loyalty. They are the end result of leadership thinking and behavior. Compromise in any way can pull one or more of the outcomes from the no-compromise zone right into the fiery pits of hell. Part Two of the book delivers a game plan for leaders to drive and hold the four outcomes in the no-compromise zone.

- **"Until now, I never understood the dynamics of leading a culture shift."** The ultimate reward for becoming a no-compromise leader is a company-wide shift to a no-compromise culture. As I wrote in Part

Three, "Most culture shifts fail. They crumble under the weight of compromise." Culture shifts certainly do take time, but it's been a joy to see leaders begin the voyage and make significant progress. It is truly magic when leaders, managers and employees at all levels adopt "no compromise" thinking and behavior. A culture shift to no compromise is truly a rite of passage for any leader.

Yes, it is exciting to see the words in my book change the performance of leaders and their companies. More then ever, I am clear that going no compromise is no longer an option in business today. No-compromise companies will weather the economic uncertainties. Companies with cultures suffering with compromising behaviors will struggle to survive. 🦃

A culture shift to no compromise
is truly a rite of passage
for any leader.

Leadership success
is a moving target

Consider for a moment that you're exploring a new career opportunity. The job description reads something like this: "Candidates must be prepared to accept relentless change, succeed in areas outside his or her comfort zones, make decisions that will impact the livelihoods of others, work as many hours as necessary to produce measurable results, accept responsibility for the mistakes of others, be able to handle high levels of stress, know how to manage cash flow, and be held personally accountable for the success or failure of the business."

Wow, I bet you're saying to yourself, "This sounds like the job opportunity of a lifetime!" Actually, I bet you're thinking that only a nut case would take a job like that. Guess what? You're a leader and that job description is yours. (Hey, it's mine too.)

Leadership is something you can get better at, but never be perfect. This simple truth is why leadership is, and always will be, a moving target. The best leaders work hard at enhancing their leadership skills. They hire coaches to push them and hold them accountable. They live the concept of continuous improvement. The bulk of the leadership population seems to be on a quest to find the "magic pill." They do seek to improve and step up their game, but mostly when situations push them to. The rest just don't get it and find more ways to hold the title of "leader" but not do the work. They function in a world of blame and excuses. Tough stuff to read, but true.

Leadership is a moving target because of the following:

- **The enormity of relentless change:** Try as you might, it is impossible to halt change. As a leader, there are only three choices: Do nothing, go with it, or lead change. If you do nothing while the world around is changing, you and the company you lead will become irrelevant. Travel agencies did nothing and became irrelevant. Expedia and Travelocity chose to lead change. If you just go along with change, you're competing with the masses. If you lead change, your competition becomes irrelevant. You stay focused on the moving target while others lose sight of it.

- **The double whammy:** It's one thing to lead a company to success, but to simultaneously develop as a leader adds complexity. This is especially so for entrepreneurs. It's common to see a business grow beyond the abilities of its leader. Given this, the aspirations of many leaders to take their companies to the next level will never be fulfilled if they choose to stop growing as a leader. Note that I used the word "choose." Self-development and achieving one's full potential as a leader, or anything else in life, is a choice.

- **The people factor:** Leading people and creating dynamic business cultures are more complex and challenging than many leaders ever imagined. That's why some leaders who excel at start-ups and turnaround situations struggle once the excitement of the challenge is behind them. In contrast, other leaders are amazing at refining and growing solid companies. Only an impressive few are capable of doing both. The dynamics of leading people to achieve a shared vision in a variety of business situations will always remain a process of continuous leadership development.

Leadership is something you can get better at, but never be perfect.

Pat yourself on the back for being a leader. You play the leading role in your own success story. If you want the ending to show you standing on the top of the mountain, you must accept the truth that leadership is a moving target. Only those who are relentlessly focused on the target will climb that mountain. Those who don't will only get so far – but at least they tried. And there will always be those who dream of climbing the mountain, but never take that first step. Keep the moving target of leadership in sight and you're bound to hit the bull's-eye.

Every leader's internal battle

As leader, it's your job to achieve the right outcomes in every part of the company. I call them the Four Business Outcomes: productivity, profitability, staff retention and customer loyalty. In just a few words, I defined the role of leader. If only being a leader was that easy. It's not. Leadership is hard. Leadership is a roller coaster of emotional highs and lows, wins and losses, joy and tears. And within every leader, a battle rages between heart and mind. The heart represents emotions. The mind represents clarity and logic. Together, they mix about as well as oil and water.

To understand the complexity of the battle between heart and mind, consider what happens when you need to make a tough decision. Tough decisions (mind) always impact the lives of others (heart). Consider how you feel when your mind is telling you that the performance of someone you really like just isn't where it needs to be and there are no signs that it ever will be. Your mind is telling you exactly what to do. Your heart is fighting back with all of the emotions of a potential lost friendship, how it may break his or her spirit, the financial hardship of a loss of income and all the drama and negativity that may surround your decision. To ignore the situation is a compromise. To go "no compromise" is hard.

What if, like medications, leadership came with a warning list of side effects? "If you choose to accept this job, you may experience extreme stress, anxiety, negativity, disdain from others, and other gut-wrenching experiences." Would you have taken the job? Of course you would – just as you take medications knowing the side effects.

- **Recognize it early:** You can feel when your heart and mind begin to battle. When you allow the battle to rage on, it dials up internal stress that's almost impossible to conceal. By recognizing it early, you can position whatever triggered the battle as a task to address. It doesn't matter how complex the matter is, it is a task that found its way onto your plate. Tasks require you to assess, plan and execute on a timeline. Heart and mind battles are less stressful when recognized and managed early.

- **Get it off your plate:** It's one thing to recognize and acknowledge the battle. It's another to get it off your plate. Your mind wants a resolution. Your heart wants to argue each and every "what if." The longer the battle continues, the more disruptive and damaging it gets. No-compromise leaders are compassionate and caring – but their ultimate accountability is to the health of the company. This means finding a balance between heart and mind to arrive at a resolution. The heart keeps the resolution from being rushed. The mind keeps it from lingering on. The longer it stays on your plate, the more it distracts you and everyone else in the company from doing great work.

- **Please the company first:** If you please the company first, you can please everyone else - employees, customers, vendors and the community. I see too many leaders get caught up in what others want (heart) and the company pays the price. FACT: Leaders can't please everyone all of the time. Not every decision will be greeted with shouts of joy. There will be times when unpopular decisions are best for the company. No-compromise leaders are prepared to make those decisions because only a healthy and enduring company can take care of everyone who depends on it.

- **Know your center:** There are leaders who are all about the results (mind). There are leaders who are compassionate to the core (heart). And there are no-compromise leaders who seek a balance between both extremes. The gravity or nature of a situation may cause your center to shift. At times, more compassion is the best course. Other times may require the clarity of logic. It's what makes you human and real. But knowing how far to shift from center is what defines you as a leader.

- **Wins and losses:** I've made some pretty darn good decisions over the years, and I've had my share of bloopers. I believe that the best decisions were made when my heart and mind were working together rather than against each other. Leaders make decisions. That's our job. Keeping the internal battle between heart and mind under control is the best strategy to rack up more wins than losses. The good news is that your heart will forgive you when you make a blooper. 🐓

Lions and tigers and bears – Oh my!

What are you afraid of? How do I know you're afraid? It's because I know how entrepreneurs and leaders get stuck when confronted with tough decisions. If you say, "I'm not afraid of anything," then answer this question: Why haven't you made that tough decision that's been waiting months for you to make? You know, the decision that will have a profound impact on your company. A decision that will stop the bleeding or eliminate obstacles to success. One that will result in significant breakthroughs.

So, what are you really afraid of? What's the absolute worst thing that can happen if you make those tough decisions? Maybe you'll be unpopular and upset some people – but you won't upset everyone. Maybe you'll lose some customers. Maybe you'll lose some employees – but was that going to happen anyway? Maybe the extent of your financial crisis will come out in the open – but chances are that most already know. Maybe you'll blow up the company – but is it headed in that direction already?

The four truths about making the toughest leadership decisions:

1. **The outcome you fear most is rarely as bad you imagined.** The simple process of working through a tough decision prepares you for most of the stuff you dread – if that stuff occurs at all. I'm not suggesting that your toughest decisions will be pain-free or stress-free, I'm just stating that the resilience of the human spirit to adapt and overcome will prevail. But it can only prevail if you engage. This leads me to truth number two.

2. **Avoiding the tough decisions can be pure agony.** The longer you wait, the more stressful it gets. The longer you wait, the more difficult the solution or change. This leads to number three.

3. **Avoid the tough decision entirely and you'll get to personally meet those lions and tigers and bears.** Tough decisions are easy to obsess over. You get bogged down in the "what if" mode. Even if your worst fear is that you'll lose everything, making tough decisions is your

responsibility. Team members are looking to you to make them, to lead them and to show the way. Fail this most basic leadership responsibility and you'll lose the support and respect of your team. Doing nothing is an open invitation to all of your worst fears.

4. **Total commitment is non-negotiable.** You must be committed to seeing through the implementation of your tough decisions. You must be committed to adjusting course when necessary to ensure the intended destination is reached. Quitting is a direct path to the lions and tigers and bears.

Too many leaders are so consumed by the potential outcomes of tough decisions that nothing changes. The road to success is not a highway. It's a complex maze of unexpected detours, potholes and roadblocks. Relish those times when you're on a clear stretch of road because new twists and turns are just around the bend.

The road to success is not a highway.
It's a complex maze
of unexpected detours, potholes and roadblocks.

You can't dance with the elephant in your business

It's time to acknowledge that there is an elephant in your business. More importantly, no matter how hard you try, it is impossible to dance with that elephant. The elephant is all about that "thing" that's been eating away at you and your business. The elephant is that big issue or problem you've been trying to maneuver around but not touch. It's there, and no matter how hard you try to move around your elephant, it just won't go away.

Confused? Then you're still refusing to acknowledge your elephant's presence. So much so that you've gotten used to moving around it. Having your elephant in the way for so long feels almost normal. Yet, it's a source of great stress. All that maneuvering wears you down and drains resources. The elephant needs to go away. And its removal falls squarely on your shoulders.

So what does this elephant look like?

- **Your company's payroll is too high and no longer sustainable:** Maybe you moved around it by cutting your own pay. Maybe you put a payroll or two on your personal credit card. (Yes, these days, this desperate measure is more common than you think.) Removing this elephant may require implementing a new pay system. It may mean that you must lay off people. It may mean changing your lifestyle. Stop dancing around your elephant.

- **Employees are not performing:** If they're not performing, how long have you been suffering from a case of intolerable toleration? Are you afraid that key employees will quit if you start holding them accountable? The elephant is your fear of addressing behaviors that you enabled by not engaging. Be the leader that your company needs and have the conversations that you've been avoiding. If someone quits, so be it. Get rid of the elephant.

- **You're stuck in yesterday:** If there's any lesson this recent recession is teaching leaders, it's that the game of business has changed and will continue to change at a rapid pace. What brought you success yesterday probably won't bring you success tomorrow. Yesterday's manner of doing business is the elephant. It's in your way and holding you back. Let go of yesterday. Try something crazy. Something fun. Something bold. Innovative action is the best eviction notice for an elephant.

These are times for no-compromise leaders to show their stuff. Be courageous. Recognize that dancing around your elephant is draining money and resources. More importantly, the stress and anxiety are a detriment to your personal wellbeing. Stop dancing and evict your elephant. 🐘

Yesterday's
manner of doing business
is the elephant.
It's in your way and
holding you back.
Let go of yesterday.

You can't lead a company walking on eggshells

Whenever you bring a group of people together, a natural leader emerges. You've seen it played out on TV shows, such as "Survivor." One player steps up and takes control of the game, becoming a de facto leader. It's different in business. One might assume that the leader of an organization is the entrepreneur with the courage and resources to start the business and turn a vision into reality. Is this entrepreneur a natural leader? Only time will tell. An employee may stand out from the pack and change the course of the business. Is this person a natural leader? Again, only time will tell.

Leaders get projects across the finish line. They know how to define and communicate the destination. They rally their teams for the cause. They challenge and inspire people to stretch to be the best. Their integrity and accountability create and maintain trust. Great leaders come in all sorts of packages from gregarious and demanding to reserved and nurturing. But the common denominator is their ability to make decisions and get things done.

When a leader constantly walks on eggshells, afraid of making unpopular or tough decisions, things get complicated. The business slows down. Uncertainty, drama and speculation permeate the work environment. The wrong behaviors go unchecked until they become the norm. Drama and funk occur waiting for the leader to step off the eggshells, assume control and point the company in the right direction. Eggshell leaders are rarely natural leaders. Most, however, have enough leadership qualities to be an effective leader – if they can avoid the "walking on eggshells" syndrome.

- **Learn to identify the first "crunch":** The moment you hear the first crunch of eggshells, it signals that you are allowing your personal emotions, insecurities or fears to take you out of leadership mode. Leading is not about you; it's about doing what's best for the company and your employees. Keep off the eggshells.

- **You can't please everyone:** This is perhaps the most common trap. Decisions need to be made. Change must occur. And, as sure as the sun rises every day, there will be one or more team members who balk at or resist your decision. Just remember, change resisters are typically few in number. Most will support and even welcome the change, as long as they understand what the possible outcomes will look like. If you cave into the few, you will be compromising the many. Keep off the eggshells.

- **Never compromise the company's vision:** It doesn't matter if you're the owner of the company, its designated president or the head of a work group, you are the leader who is responsible for ensuring the health, vitality, stability and growth of the company. Even if it means the painful decision to shrink the company so it can grow better, you're the keeper of the company's vision. Keep off the eggshells.

When a leader constantly
walks on eggshells,
afraid of making
unpopular or tough decisions,
things get complicated.

- **Grow into your role as leader:** Every company is unique. Each has its challenges and internal drama. No matter what your previous leadership experience is, you still have a lot to learn. You still have insecurities to overcome. You still need to find the courage to make decisions that will impact the lives and livelihoods of others. And you will gain the wisdom of a leader. You will grow into your role. Keep off the eggshells.

Ask the right questions

The question most often asked during a recession is: "When will it end?" It's the natural tendency for a return to business as usual. But as the economy shows signs of recovery, prudent leaders are asking extremely tough questions. Rather than slipping back into old leadership patterns, they're asking how they must change as leaders to adapt to what is clearly a new and challenging economic reality. If you think that stress levels will dial down, your thinking is going to lead you down a dangerous path that doesn't end in the "happy days" of yesteryear.

Although there were clear signs in 2008 that a recession was looming, the economy tanked so fast that many businesses were caught off guard and unprepared for rough times. Savvy leaders engaged promptly to cut expenses and plug financial leaks. Leaders who acted quickly and decisively faired better. Those who hesitated felt the pain of weakened sales and poorly controlled spending. Whatever the economic reality, leaders must take stock of where they are and must be willing to face the truth about their leadership successes and challenges.

- **How do you need to change as a leader?** Where did your leadership style fall short? Did your tendency to be a friend and well-liked leader make it difficult for you to shift into a focused and decisive mode? Did your command-and-control style keep your leadership team from helping you create and implement needed changes? Did your hands-off style have your leadership floundering as they waited for their leader to engage?

- **What leadership skills are you lacking?** No leader is a complete package. What's missing in your leadership toolbox? Is it time to get a handle on cash-flow management? Are your communication skills lacking? Are your time management skills deficient? Are you a master of procrastination?

- **What systems misfired? What systems are missing?** You lead people – you manage systems. That's the magic formula. If you don't like the outcomes you're getting in any area of your business, it's time to examine, upgrade or build entirely new systems to achieve the results you want.

- **Is your company culture contaminated?** It can be agonizingly stressful to rally a team that has trust issues, internal drama, entitlement thinking and no sense of urgency. If your culture is contaminated, get help. A culture shift requires a thorough understanding of what no-compromise leadership is all about.

> If you don't like the outcomes you're getting in any area of your business, **it's time to examine, upgrade or build entirely new systems** to achieve the results you want.

- **What's innovative about your company?** Nothing fires a company up than a major initiative. Take a brutally honest look at your company. If all you see is the same old stuff and activity, it's time for some innovative thinking to invigorate your company, its people and its culture.

Great leaders look at and anticipate what their companies need beyond the horizon. When emerging from tough times, they ask the right questions about what needs to change. They learn, grow and mature as leaders. The process never ends.

Dictatorial and inflexible or determined and resolute

While discussing leadership blockages (those situations and accountabilities where procrastination and avoidance surface) at a No-Compromise Leadership Boot Camp, the group got stuck on the fine line that separates a dictatorial and inflexible mode from being determined and resolute. If a leader says, "This is the way it needs to be done," which mode is he or she leading in? Interestingly, it all depends on the thinking and behavior of individual leaders – and the situation in question.

If a leader is implementing a new system to dramatically fix and improve the customer-service experience – and is holding team members accountable – is this being dictatorial or resolute? If it's a system that everyone was trained on, agreed to and is good for the customer, the answer is resolute. If an employee is violating a standard of performance – or something as basic as dress code – is holding the employee accountable being dictatorial or resolute? Again, the answer is resolute.

In contrast, if the leader says, "This is the way it needs to be done," and gives no explanation to clarify his or her intentions and refuses any collaboration, this is being dictatorial and inflexible. This is the infamous, "my way or the highway" tactic that does more to demoralize people and contaminate a culture.

- **Is it good for the customer?** If it's good for the customer, it gets done. When a leader allows systems, procedures and quality issues to go unaddressed, compromise contaminates the culture. A leader cannot allow negative behavior to compromise the customer loyalty business outcome.

- **Clarify your intentions and expectations:** Let employees know the entire story and how you and the entire team must be accountable. Most of all, explain how you will hold everyone accountable.

- **Work through your blockages:** If you're quick to label a situation that requires you to be determined and resolute as being dictatorial and inflexible, think "compromise" or "no compromise." Is the situation or person compromising the integrity of the company? Then you must be determined and resolute and engage as the leader. If you feel yourself hesitating or avoiding, think "compromise" or "no compromise." No compromise must become your leadership mantra.

Leaders create unnecessary drag when they hesitate or avoid addressing issues and situations because they perceive it as being dictatorial and inflexible. The role of the no-compromise leader is to protect the integrity of the company culture, and to do so with integrity and respect.

The role of the
no-compromise leader is to
**protect the integrity
of the company culture,**
and to do so with
integrity and respect.

Are you keeping the commitments you make?

Here's one of my favorite Neilisms: Do you do quarterly performance evaluations at least once a year? As amusing as it sounds, it addresses the fundamental issue that plagues too many business leaders: the casual breaking of commitments. It can be something as innocent as being late for a meeting or forgetting to respond to an employee request, all the way up to the big stuff, such as promising a pay review or promotion. FACT: A broken commitment wrecks trust. In our coaching practice, we consistently find that the root cause of employee turnover, backroom banter, resistance to change and outright distrust of leadership is driven by broken commitments. Here's a quick checklist to help you stay on top of your commitments:

- **Stop blaming others for not trusting you.** There are always reasons, and it's your responsibility to initiate dialogue to discover what you can do to regain trust.

- **Think before you commit.** If you're casual about making commitments, chances are that you fail to keep many of them. Always ask yourself, "Can I really fulfill this commitment to the best of my ability and do so on time?"

- **Manage what's on your plate.** Learn to recognize when your plate is full and that it's OK to say, "I can't take this on right now," or, "Let's set a date to discuss how we can get this done."

- **View every commitment as a contract.** Schedule a meeting – be there. Promise to call someone back this afternoon – make that call. Take on a project – get it done right and on time. Your reputation is on the line every time.

- **Manage expectations.** Get all the issues and concerns on the table from the start. If you feel the commitment will take longer to fulfill than you'd like, say so. If you're stuck, ask for help. If you know you're going to miss a deadline, give advance warning as early as you can – but don't make it a habit.

- **Even the tiniest commitment needs clarity.** Be certain you understand the details of what you're committing to. Ask questions. Repeat what you believe the commitment to be to ensure you've got it right. Clarity first – commitment second.

- **Be the first to make a broken commitment right.** No exceptions. No compromise.

The root cause of
employee turnover,
backroom banter,
resistance to change and
outright distrust of leadership
is driven by
broken commitments.

Confronting confrontation

I would never want to encounter a leader frothing at the mouth, wandering around like a mad dog looking for confrontation. And if by chance I did, I would never tolerate or subject myself to such demeaning and abusive behavior. Confrontation just isn't something that most people seek out. There isn't anything about confrontation that feels good. Yet, it's something that leaders have to deal with. The question is: How do you confront confrontation?

"I don't like confrontation." That's something leaders tell me all the time. My response is always, "Who does?" However, dealing effectively with confrontation is an ability leaders need to make peace with. In a leadership role, the first step is to accept confrontation for what it is: a conversation that seeks to resolve a problem or situation that has the potential to become emotional. Add one more essential element: It is a conversation that must be done without procrastination.

- **You are the voice of the company:** It's your job to speak on behalf of your company. When you avoid, procrastinate, or engage in the conversation but candy-coat the issue, you are compromising the wellbeing of the company, its employees and customers. Engaging in difficult conversations is what you signed on for when you accepted the role of leader.

- **It's not about you:** If you get a ticket for speeding, you were speeding. The police officer gave you a speeding ticket because you chose to speed. When dealing with behavior or performance issues, you are addressing the chosen behaviors of employees who compromise the standards and culture of the company. Don't make it personal.

- **Keep the conversation safe:** It's natural to anticipate that an employee will negatively react during a confrontational conversation. When the conversation begins, you're looking for that anticipated reaction which can trigger a more aggressive response from you. It's like a trap you set for yourself. When the conversation gets aggressive on either side, the natural reaction is "fight or flight." And that's when things get ugly. It's your job to keep the conversation safe and focused on achieving the desired outcome.

- **Avoid "I-just-want-to-get-it-over-with" thinking:** Of course you want to get the conversation over with. But you can't keep the conversation "safe" when your tactic is to drop a bomb and see what happens. These conversations take time, so give them time.

- **So, you like to procrastinate:** Here's a Neilism: "Giving into a leadership blockage today gives you a bigger problem tomorrow." Avoiding confrontational conversations is what I call a leadership blockage. The longer you avoid a problem, the bigger it gets. And the bigger it gets, the more emotional and volatile the conversation can become. No-compromise leadership means, "If it needs to be done – get it done."

Engaging in **difficult conversations** is what you signed on for when you accepted the role of leader.

- **Flip it:** Simply changing your perspective to coaching can help you work through a confrontational conversation. Help an employee reach his or her full potential by coaching them. "Stop doing that" is not coaching. Asking an employee how he or she could have approached a situation differently and discussing alternatives feels a whole lot better than initiating a verbal battle.

- **And then there are those tough ones:** Yes, there will be those conversations that fail to reach the desired resolution. They become heated and don't end well. These are learning opportunities to grow as a leader. No-compromise leaders aren't perfect, but they sure try to get better every day. 🐔

How to motivate employees

You're working hard to drive your company forward. You have customers to keep happy, vendors to maintain relationships with, myriad financial pressures, plus all the thrills and chills of leading employees. You might want to view employees as a dynamic yet unstable mass of energy that requires constant attention to produce the desired outcomes. Just when you think you've got everything dialed in just right, something simple can disturb the balance and cause things to go haywire.

Sometimes that mass of energy can become so slow and lifeless that progress grinds to a halt. That's when leaders begin scratching their heads and praying to the leadership gods for the answer to the ultimate business question: How do you motivate employees? Why is the answer so elusive and complex? Easy: We're dealing with an extraordinary concoction of personalities, thinking and behaviors. Motivators that work for some never work for all. And, just when you think you have the balance and energy right, the slightest lack of attention, appreciation, drama or loss of focus can throw a motivated team into a whining and grumbling funk.

- **Give them something to fight for:** People will go the extra mile for a cause that touches their hearts and minds. Hey, it could even be, "We have to do this to survive and save our jobs." It could be the goal to have the best year ever and hit bonus. It could be working together to build something extraordinary for a special client. Projects, innovation, raising money for a charity, anything that aligns the energy of a team on a goal. That's what motivates people.

- **Knock off the command-and-control tactics:** Fear is a short-term motivator. It may get a job done, but it does nothing to build a dynamic culture. The flipside of command and control is mentoring, coaching, clarifying expectations, communication, acknowledgement and opportunity. Reprimands certainly do have their place, but if your style is 80-percent reprimand and 20-percent positive reinforcement, don't expect inspired motivation to magically materialize in your company.

- **An unmotivated leader can't motivate anyone:** Leading and growing a business can wear you down as a leader. If you take enough hits without a win, it can be hard to put your game face on and inspire others. Leaders need to monitor their own emotional state and know when to ask for help. The worst thing a leader can do is to try to carry the weight of the entire company on his or her shoulders. There are team members who really care and will step up. And the best leaders rely on the guidance and encouragement of a coach or mentor. That outside perspective is invaluable because they can see solutions and opportunities that you cannot.

So, the secret sauce to motivating people is, and always will be, in the hands of the leader. Are you asking the question, "How do you motivate people?" Then, it's time to step back and assess your approach to leadership. 🐓

The worst thing a leader can do is to try to carry **the weight of the entire company** on his or her shoulders.

Communicating without words

You're really engrossed in your work and an employee interrupts and asks, "Do you have a minute?" You look away from your work, make eye contact and acknowledge the request with an affirmative nod. The employee launches off into a story that rabbit-trails down so many paths that you become frustrated and stop listening. You roll your eyes, tighten your lips with a big sigh. The employee sees that you're annoyed and not interested in what she has to say. The conversation ends.

The employee now feels unimportant and insignificant – like a discarded possession. She heads over to some co-worker friends and says, "He just didn't care about what I had to say; he didn't even listen." You didn't utter a word, but you spoke volumes. It's the oldest form of communication. It's called body language.

While teaching at a seminar, I was into a segment of the course that always has attendees asking questions. It was one of the business concepts that push leaders out of their comfort zones. I love the questions as it really engages everyone in the class.

After the seminar ended, I sat down to read over the comment sheets. High scores and accolades are always nice, but it's the constructive criticism that helps you improve and grow. One comment sheet said, "I was really put off when I asked Neil a question and he rolled his eyes."

Wow. I had no idea I even did that. Maybe I just looked up to contemplate my response. Maybe I was frustrated with myself that it was taking longer to get my point across. Maybe I just rolled my eyes. The reason doesn't matter. A good customer was put off by my non-verbal communication. I'm more aware now and regard the criticism as a gift. But it still bothers me, and I do own it.

We engage in non-verbal communication almost every waking moment. We're reading other people's body language too. And I'm sure we can agree that there are times where our body language is telling the truth about how we feel even when our words don't.

As a leader, you need to be aware of what you're communicating at all times. Here are some simple suggestions to avoid sending the wrong message through your body language:

- **Avoid multi-tasking:** If you're working on something that needs your attention and you're interrupted, you can't give your full attention to anything else until you stop. If you attempt to do both, you will compromise both. If you can't accommodate the interruption, the best course is to say, "What you have to say is important and I want to give you my full attention. Can we meet in an hour?"

- **Be present:** If your thoughts are drifting elsewhere, your body language will indicate you're disconnected. The most common infraction is when you start constructing your response while others are speaking. Listening requires concentration. It's difficult, if not impossible, to fake attentive listening. The best course is to listen with the intent of clarifying what you just heard. It sounds something like, "From what you're telling me, the challenge you're having is …"

It's difficult, if not impossible, **to fake attentive listening.**

- **Control your body:** This is easier said than done. Your eyes, breathing, lips, head rolling, posture, arms, hands and legs all speak. You can appear defensive, insulted, annoyed, bored, indifferent – even hostile. Or, if you pay attention and remain aware of what you're body is saying, you can appear engaged, supportive, concerned, proud, happy – and caring. Sit up straight and lean into the conversation rather than back away. Maintain eye contact. If you're having a conversation that you know will be emotional on one or both sides, avoid gestures and postures like the rolling eyes, crossed arms, pointing of fingers and other body language that is meant to intimidate.

- **Leadership demeanor:** It is so easy for a leader to alter the positive mood of a business by appearing worried, angry or under excessive stress. It sounds like, "Our fearless leader is in one of those moods; watch out." Leaders are "on stage" all day, every day. Their words and body language can instill confidence, excitement and energy, or fear, concern, doom and gloom. When leaders arrive at work, they need to be centered, grounded and aware of everything they're communicating. It's the work of leadership.

Ask some employees how they read your body language. Share how you read theirs. Then, consider a company-wide exploration of how customers read everyone's body language. It can be most enlightening. ☙

Our body language
is telling the truth
about how we feel
even when
our words don't.

*Where's the sense
of urgency?*

Leave nothing unsaid

You're getting ready to do a performance evaluation with a key employee. There are some behavior and performance issues that surfaced a while back that you had hoped were temporary and would just fade away. But, as they often do, the issues continued and now they are beginning to impact other members of your team. You know this employee is highly sensitive to constructive feedback, and the process often produces all kinds of drama, emotions and funk. Because of this, getting into the tough stuff with this employee always produces a knot in your stomach.

So, the evaluation begins. You navigate through the process until you reach that point where all that remains is the tough stuff. You feel as though you've cornered a wild beast, and you're trying to find the best moment and angle to capture it without getting mauled. And then it happens – you ask the employee if she has any questions, and you end the evaluation. You hesitated. You left essential things unsaid. You wimped out. You compromised.

This scenario gets played out in business every day. You notice behavior and performance issues, and you fail to engage. Interestingly, it only occurs with certain individuals when your pre-conceived mental picture of the process and the immediate fallout cranks up your anxiety levels high enough to hit the compromise button. To make matters worse, you beat yourself up for missing the opportunity to address a growing problem that will only continue to escalate.

- **Just get it over with:** When it comes to confronting reality and dealing with the tough stuff, if you hesitate, you lose. That's it. Address it and move on. Lingering issues do more damage to the performance of the business.

- **Focus on the desired outcome:** It's easy to get stuck in the emotions and stress of addressing highly sensitive and seemingly explosive issues. Help yourself and the employee by focusing attention on the desired outcome. Doing so gives purpose to the process. Addressing the tough stuff today will create a better tomorrow.

- **How bad does it get before you engage?** Here's the real kicker. If you've observed and even acknowledged that a behavior and performance problem exists and did nothing, you compromised your leadership role. If you engage when the problem surfaces, the probability of it going critical is greatly minimized.

- **What's the worse that could happen?** OK, the employee may get so upset that he or she quits. Is that a bad thing? Typically when behaviors and performance head south, the ripple effect can degrade performance and create distractions throughout a department or even the entire company. If your respectful efforts to help an employee grow and prosper are met with a resignation, consider it a favor. Accept the resignation and open the windows to allow fresh air in.

One of the most challenging aspects of being a no-compromise leader is the ability to engage in open and constructive dialogue with employees on behavior and performance issues – and to do so when the issues surface. Hesitate today and you'll just have a bigger problem tomorrow.

> When it comes to
> **confronting reality**
> and dealing with
> the tough stuff,
> if you hesitate,
> you lose.

When personal relationships compromise leadership thinking

It happens to all leaders. You've become friends with an employee. (Or, to make matters more sensitive, the employee is a relative.) Performance and/or behavior issues are becoming obvious to the rest of the team and they're looking to you for a solution. You've seen the issues for quite some time and you've had several "light" conversations with the employee hoping things would get better. Well, they haven't – and your continued reluctance to have a serious conversation is talking its toll on the team and your credibility as a leader.

When leaders allow personal relationships to cloud and distort their thinking, compromise is always the outcome. I'm not suggesting that you discard your sense of compassion and respect for your employees. Not in the least. What I am emphatically suggesting is that, as leader of your company, your prime objective is to serve and protect the integrity of the business, its team and its customers. The no-compromise leader must never see and acknowledge a problem and fail to act. Allowing a personal relationship to get in the way of action signals to every employee that you support and protect a double-standard culture – one for friends and relatives and another for everybody else. Talk about contaminating a business culture from the top down.

- **When hiring a friend or relative, establish clear expectations and guidelines, so that all employees are held to the same standards of performance.** No exceptions. No special treatment. No compromise.

- **For friends or relatives already employed, it's time for a crucial conversation that establishes where personal relationships end and business relationships and accountability begins.** Get it all out for discussion. Your goal is to have extreme clarity on how your relationships will not interfere in your ability to lead the company.

- **Have friends or relatives report to another leader.** Do not interfere. Do not override that leader's decisions. All parties will be better served though this separation.

- **If it's already gotten out of hand, it's time to fix what your compromising created.** Remember, all eyes are upon you. Your leadership credibility is on the line. Acknowledge that you allowed a double standard to evolve and that it has created issues and resentment with the rest of the team. Clearly identify what needs to change.

- **The toughest fix is when the friend or relative is in a decision-making position that he or she is clearly not qualified for.** To allow this to continue is clearly a serious compromise. In addition to the host of issues that occur when an employee is in over his or her head, it's setting the employee up for failure. Either find another position more suited to the employee's skill set or end it. You'll be doing all parties a great service.

Leadership is tough work and, on occasion, you will find yourself in the midst of a disconcerting dilemma purely of your own making. Recognize it. Fix it. For the no-compromise leader, there is no other alternative. 🐾

When leaders allow
personal relationships
**to cloud and distort
their thinking,**
compromise
is always
the outcome.

What's on your compromise list?

Every leader has one. It's that list of projects, tasks and/or responsibilities that you prefer to avoid, ignore or bestow with your highest level of procrastination. It is truly amazing how you can find a zillion other low-level things to do rather than tackle your compromise list and check off a few items. Whether it's from human nature, fear of the unknown, insecurity, lack of knowledge or skill, or just plain laziness, it's a sure bet that items lingering on your compromise list are creating drag, inefficiency, lost opportunities and increased costs in your company. Even with the knowledge of the consequences, you just can't seem to convert your compromise list into a no-compromise list of must-do items that get done.

- **Confront your list head on:** Get your emotions out of the way and take a hard look at that list. What's really on that list that you can't do? Chances are that you have sufficient skills and knowledge to do every item. If you don't, you certainly can tap the resources and expertise of others. Simply put, you can blow up your compromise list if you want to. No compromise.

- **Knock off the easiest ones first:** There's nothing like the feeling of accomplishment that comes from crossing a completed task off a challenging to-do list. By tackling the easier tasks, you'll gain momentum. The question is when will you start? No compromise.

- **There's power in the tough ones:** Think about it. It's those big ugly items on your list that really cause you discomfort and keep you up at night. It may be tough decisions like cutting hours or staff, or having that crucial conversation with a toxic employee. Whatever it is, there's power in those tasks, and by tackling them head on, you're taking control of the situation. You're doing the work of leadership. And when completed, you'll realize that it wasn't so bad and that your stress level is back under control. These days, a leader cannot avoid making difficult decisions. No compromise.

- **You're human, not Superman:** I always advise leaders to manage what's on their plates. Leadership is not about doing it all; it's about creating the right business outcomes. That leaves plenty of room to engage others in tasks, projects and responsibilities. No compromise.

- **You just may have fun:** Getting rid of your compromise list is a worthy and doable quest that will recharge you as a leader. And if you find yourself having fun in the process, you'll just have to make peace with that. No compromise. 🐾

Getting rid
of your compromise list
is a worthy and doable quest
that will recharge you
as a leader.

Present a 'state of the company' address

Every January, the president of the United States gives a State of the Union address to a joint session of Congress. The address not only reports on the condition of the nation but also allows the president to outline his legislative agenda and national priorities. Given the ongoing economic turmoil, you may wish to present a State of the Company address.

Every business and employee has been affected in some way by the recent recession. It is likely that you made some tough decisions to ensure the wellbeing of your company. Expenses were cut, projects were put on hold, and employees may have been laid off. Even on a limited scale, such decisions send unsettling vibrations throughout a company culture as employees contemplate that most fundamental question: How will this affect me?

Strategically, presenting a State of the Company address has the potential to reinvigorate your company's performance by sharing with all employees exactly what the state of the company is and how making tough decisions is allowing it to weather this economic storm. It provides you with the perfect platform to share your vision and leadership agenda for growing the company. This is all about information flow and allowing your team to have absolute clarity on where the company is going.

- **Find the right setting for the address:** Do not hold the address where you normally hold meetings. The president has the distinguished podium in the House of Representatives. You need to select a site that communicates the importance of this address. Is there a meeting room at City Hall that you can rent? Does your local college or high school have an auditorium you can use? Is there a company in your area that has a training facility available? If all else fails and you have to use your facility, hang red, white and blue banners around the space. Don't forget to get a podium.

- **The announcement to employees:** Send or hand every employee an invitation to attend your State of the Company address. Design and print a folded invitation that looks official. You can even put one of those gold foil stickers on it and imprint your corporate seal on it. (You rarely get to use that seal so now's your chance.)

- **Prepare your speech:** The president has speechwriters and edits it until the address is perfect. If you're not good at writing speeches, ask for help. You will find accomplished speechwriters at colleges and PR firms. Work on your speech and keep refining it. If it doesn't go through at least six revisions, it's not done. Rehearse and rehearse some more.

- **Dress "presidential":** You want to look like a leader. Put a lot of thought into how you want to appear to your employees for what could be the most important address to your staff.

- **Keep the entire event "official":** This isn't a party. No food. No music. Keep the entire evening official. Don't forget to have someone introduce you. This is all about nurturing and reinforcing your company culture.

This is all about
information flow
and allowing your team
to have
absolute clarity
on where
the company
is going.

No-compromise resolutions

Every so often, it's valuable to evaluate where you've been for the past several months and what you want your business to look like going forward. Don't wait until the New Year to make and keep no-compromise resolutions.

1. **Always put people before profit.** Period. Do that, lead them with passion, trust them to do the right thing, give them the freedom to do it, help them have fun, and the profit will come.

2. **Listen and really hear what employees have to say.** They are the front line of your business that customers see. They hold the insights to make things better. Respond to their suggestions and make them feel valuable.

3. **Always clarify expectations.** People need to know where they stand and where they are going. Paint a high-definition picture of your desired outcome, then establish progress checkpoint dates and times. Start each day or shift with a huddle. Provide positive and constructive feedback at every turn. Share the information they need to do their jobs.

4. **Create equality and fairness by eliminating double standards.** This means the same rules that apply to your team apply to you and that all team members are treated the same. It also means you and all team members will roll up their sleeves and pitch in when needed and that you never talk about, gossip about or degrade an employee to others.

5. **Tackle the tough stuff before it gets out of hand.** Right now, you know exactly what's on that short list of problems and issues your company needs to address. Address and fix them now because it's easier to stamp out a matchstick than a blazing forest fire.

6. **Never put off a critical conversation – even if it's outside of your comfort zone.** When you avoid or fail to act on an issue or problem, you are dealing with a leadership blockage. Acting from emotion can interfere with your ability to see and confront reality and lead to great

frustration on both sides. Once you do, you'll wonder why you waited so long.

7. **Raise the bar on customer service to the highest rung.** Customer loyalty comes from delivering extraordinary service, quality and value with a no-compromise passion. No matter what business you are in, customer loyalty drives the true growth leaders. It starts by listening to your customers and your front-line team. Never accept inferior performance or poor quality service. Your customers will notice, whether or not they tell you.

8. **Protect the financial integrity of the company.** Accountability at all levels of the company to adhere to its financial control systems is the determining factor of your company's profitability performance. You need to create a cash-flow projection, to live your plan, to pay attention to all your financial reports, to understand your financials, build cash reserves and manage debt. Unite no-compromise leadership with accountability and you will ensure balance in your profitability business outcome.

Strengthen, nurture and protect **your business culture** from contamination at all costs.

9. **Achieve maximum consistency through accountability to your systems.** Systems give your business predictability. They reduce the chances of things going awry, spinning out of control or otherwise becoming more stressful than necessary.

10. **Create a no-compromise culture that is pure world class.** Strengthen, nurture and protect your business culture from contamination at all costs. Great leaders aren't great because they're innovative, understand numbers or have good communication skills. They're great because they design, build and fiercely protect the cultures they are empowered to lead. 🐔

Neilism:
Compromise ensures consistently
inconsistent business outcomes.

CHAPTER

3

Making
It Happen

The problem with accountability

To hold one's self accountable. It's such a simple concept. Do what you say you're going to do. Follow the rules. Be committed to the system or process. Fulfill your obligations. Do the right thing. Step up when situations need you to step up. Never avoid or ignore what you are responsible to or for. In just a few short sentences, I've described the qualities and characteristics of a leader. I've also described what leaders hope and pray for in those they lead.

If the concept of accountability is so easy to describe, why is it something that leaders struggle with? Take a moment to speed-write a list of companies that you perceive as impressive in the way they perform and conduct business – companies whose thinking, behaviors and systems you would like emulate in your own company. What you just created is your personal list of organizations that you admire for their accountability to do what needs to be done. I call them no-compromise companies.

The problem with accountability is that it is the recipient of more lip service than action. Accountability – to do what needs to be done – requires a level of commitment and discipline that many leaders spend time and energy seeking ways to avoid. Every leader does this to some degree. But the problem is that the more a leader avoids it, the more leaks spring up throughout their company. Want proof? Speed-write a list of issues your company is facing at this very moment. Without question, every item on your list represents an accountability compromise. Systems missing or not followed. Rules broken. Commitments not faced. Responsibilities avoided. Problems ignored. Tough decisions avoided. Budgets not adhered to. Information not shared. Opportunities missed. I've got more, but you get the point.

- **Start with yourself:** The most common knee-jerk reaction to accountability issues sounds like, "They need to change..." A company's accountability thinking and behavior originates with its leaders. Before you start pointing your finger or casting blame, you must own your contribution to your company's accountability issues. You need to clean up your act first in order for others to follow.

- **Designate "accountability" as a core value:** If accountability is important to you, make it important to everyone in the company. Create an "accountability code of conduct" that bullet-points what high accountability thinking and behavior looks like in your company. Yes, you need to make this a collaborative effort with participants from every sector of your company. Here's one to get you started, "Everyone is responsible for our success."

- **Celebrate accountability thinking and behavior:** If you celebrate hitting goal, why aren't you celebrating the accountabilities that made it happen? Achieving a company goal takes discipline, commitment, teamwork, structure, organization, information flow and drive – none of which would occur in the absence of accountability. Identify it. Praise it. Reward it.

Accountability is the recipient of more **lip service** than action.

- **Stop accepting mediocrity:** Yeah, it's happening in your company every day. Mediocrity, or as I like to call it, "the relentless pursuit of average," is the by-product of indifference. Indifference is nothing more than an individual's conscious decision to perform at a level below his or her capabilities – at the expense of everyone else. When indifference collides with high accountability, it will lose every time. For this very reason, there is opportunity and growth potential that is slipping (or gushing) through the cracks because leaders compromise when it comes to accountability.

Accountability is a massive and complex topic with many twists and turns. But in the end, it all comes down to the thinking and behavior choices you make as a leader. The defining factor is whether those choices lean toward accountability or compromise. Which direction is your accountability meter leaning?

Quality's biggest flaw

Quality is a beautiful thing to experience. In a product or service, quality is evident in its innovative design, attention to detail and flawless performance. From iPhones and iPads, to fine hotels and restaurants, to automobiles and jetliners, the presence of quality is evident – even expected and demanded. The pursuit of quality has been at the forefront of business thinking since post World War II and the work of W. Edwards Deming. Systems, processes and measurements eliminate flaws to deliver consistent quality.

Yet, with all the gains in delivering consistent quality, consider the millions of cars that Toyota recalled in 2010 due to flaws. Consider the Hubble Space Telescope that was painstakingly designed and built – and launched into space with flawed lenses. Consider the Southwest Airline's Boeing 737 that blew a five-foot by one-foot hole in the rear of the passenger cabin at 37,000 feet. Consider that dinner that didn't live up to your expectations or that stay at a five-star hotel that delivered a three-star experience. These are all examples where quality is the mandate yet something was inherently flawed.

During a keynote address I gave at *Quality Magazine's* annual Quality Conference, I asked the audience, "What is quality's biggest flaw?" After a few moments of contemplation, I said, "People. People represent quality's biggest flaw." With that statement, I shifted their thinking from measurements and standards to the one overriding factor to achieving quality – the individuals whose thinking and behavior drives or degrades quality outcomes.

- **It's about making choices:** Behaviors are a choice. Follow the system or process, or take a shortcut. Put in the effort that quality demands, or give less than you're capable of. If the mandate is producing quality, everyone involved must be mentally and emotionally locked in to producing quality. If it was a failed bolt that caused the hole in that Southwest Airlines flight, the person making that bolt needs to know that lives depend on every bolt meeting exact specs and tolerances.

Connect thinking to the outcome and you have a better chance of the right choices being made.

- **It's about persistent feedback and information flow:** Coaches work with athletes to refine their game. Moves are analyzed and fine-tuned to improve performance. Without such persistent feedback, the athletes are left to self-monitor their performance – and over time, that performance can degrade. It is so easy for certain aspects of work to become routine, and attention to detail can skip a few beats. If some persistent feedback and information flow could have avoided the Hubble lens debacle, hundreds of millions of dollars could have been saved, and several Space Shuttle missions to fix the problem could have been avoided. If you think you're giving adequate feedback and information flow, think again. There is always room for improvement. Isn't that what quality is all about?

People represent quality's biggest flaw.

- **Leadership:** Leaders set the tone, pace, standards and emotional engagement in the pursuit of quality. Leaders who accept "average" cannot achieve quality. Leaders who accept "average" and give almost their best cannot inspire the commitment, dedication and relentless drive that produces quality. Leaders who lead their companies to deliver quality are a special breed. They represent quality in everything they do. They believe in it. They pursue it. They find the right people and resources to create it. They take ownership in achieving quality. If you're on the relentless pursuit for quality, do you possess these traits?

One last thought: Quality is not a one-time occurrence. It's consistent and can be duplicated. It endures. And for those who lead it and achieve it, it delivers a sense of fulfillment that is beyond words. ✒

The pressure test:
Manage or meltdown

Every business goes through periods of high stress. It's when varying combinations of sluggish sales, tight cash flow, employee problems, productivity issues, customer complaints and the like merge together like the weather systems in *The Perfect Storm*. Business stress can lead to what I fondly call "owners' nights" – waking up at 3:00 a.m. in a cold sweat. High-stress situations can lead to a further degrading of the issues that initiated the pressure in the first place. The inherent danger is allowing such situations to spiral out of control.

If you equate high-stress situations to a steam boiler, it's easy to see how they can lead to catastrophe. As the pressure gauge enters the red danger zone, the weakest parts of the boiler system begin to spring leaks. The steam and hissing from the leaks not only grab attention, they warn of impending disaster if not managed and contained.

Leaders and businesses are pressure tested every day. And in these stressful economic times, those pressure tests are becoming more frequent.

- **Address the weakest links now:** In most cases, you know exactly where and what they are. Cash is tight and you're not paying attention to your numbers? It's time to go no-compromise with your financial controls. Has your company's sense of urgency taken a siesta? It's time to revisit your vision, polish it up, put a pin on the win map – and lead your company to victory. Just remember, weak links are typically found in areas and accountabilities that leaders avoid or are uncomfortable digging into.

- **Make "change" a constant:** Leaks occur in organizations that experience few or no change initiatives. It's just human nature to settle in and get comfortable. That's why you always head straight for the same seat on the second day of a seminar. The opposite of change is stagnation. If your company starts springing leaks when it tries to implement even minor change, it's going to fail the pressure test. If you want a dynamic company, you must relentlessly improve your systems.

- **Speaking of systems:** Inconsistency is an indicator of missing or inadequate systems. Inconsistency guarantees a meltdown at low-pressure levels. To survive and thrive, you and your company must embrace systemization in every nook and cranny. Rest assured, creativity and innovation thrive when supported by the right systems.

- **Get it done:** Accountability is the foundation of no-compromise leadership. It's the secret sauce of world-class success. Build and nurture a no-compromise culture and the needle on the pressure-test gauge will float happily in the "normal zone."

At first, these four bullet points may seem academic, but you and I both know that work needs to be done in every one. Why? Is that a hissing sound I hear? ✆

Inconsistency is an indicator
of missing or
inadequate systems.

Synchronize a sense of urgency

Situation: You're freaking out over payroll costs and know darn well that your team is not playing to its full potential. On a scale of one to ten, your sense-of-urgency dial is slammed against the red line at ten. In contrast, your team's sense-of-urgency dial is set at the 6.5 mark; they're barely breaking a sweat. You're getting frustrated because they just don't seem to "get it." They're getting frustrated because they don't understand why you're freaking or what you want them to do. It seems the harder you push, the more stressed everyone gets. The company's sense of urgency is out of synch.

When the sense of urgency is out of synch, it's like trying to drive a car with a doughnut spare tire on one wheel, one at maximum pressure, one almost flat, and the last with just the right pressure. The car won't perform right. It can't go fast. It pulls to one side, the engine has to work harder, and it's just plain dangerous. When the sense-of-urgency dials for different segments of a company are out of synch, the company simply will not perform to its full potential.

You'll know when all the sense-of-urgency dials in your company are in synch, especially if they're all set at eight or nine. Your company will be performing like a racecar.

- **No, they don't know:** Try walking around your company and cranking up the sense of urgency. By the time you get back to your office, just about every dial will be back to where it was. Big missions, visions and worthy challenges are the greatest mechanisms to both synch and reset sense-of-urgency dials at high-performance levels. Too many leaders start by cranking up everyone's urgency dial with "we gotta do more" mandates. Start with a vision that's worthy of the quest. Give the details and unleash daily information flow to ensure understanding and progress.

- **Freight train or bullet train:** You can talk about getting to that "next level" all you want, but you'll never get there moving at the speed of "almost breaking a sweat." To move fast, your company's systems, accountability and information flow need to be up to the challenge and working in concert. Leaders must fearlessly change, modify or eliminate those elements of the company that are not working. And you know exactly what some of those elements are that need fixing. If you don't know, ask your team, they'll tell you. You can't go fast with broken or worn-out parts.

- **Know when to dial it down:** I like to challenge myself with century bike rides (100 miles). I watch riders blast off at high speed and hammer away at their pedals for the first third of the route only to find that they have nothing left for the big climbs and to cross the finish line strong. I'm not a fast rider, but I know how to pace myself so I can finish strong. Pushing your team full out without dialing down the urgency to recoup will never get you to that next level. Take time to assess and adjust to changing realities. This goes for the leader as much as for the team.

You can talk about **getting to that "next level"** all you want, but you'll never get there moving at the speed of "almost breaking a sweat."

Every company you admire for its performance and consistency has mastered the ability to synch its sense of urgency in every nook and cranny of the company. Step back and assess how all of your company's sense-of-urgency dials are set. Then, seize the opportunity. No compromise. ♘

No-compromise decisions are now in play

The trend is clear: Leaders are rising to the occasion and making some of the toughest and most gut-wrenching decisions in years. Never before have I seen such widespread and aggressive corrective measures taken to counteract the affects of the recession.

Clearly the collective psyche of business leaders has shifted into damage and prevention control at a pace that's truly unprecedented. When sales are down across the business spectrum, leaders must confront their cash-flow challenges head on. As a result, no-compromise leadership stories are apparent everywhere as leaders make the tough decisions that must be made.

It's one thing to clamp down on spending, but when cost reductions must extend to cutting hours, staff layoffs and looking to your team to do more with less, the stress and weight of leadership accountability must be managed. The no-compromise leader in you must prevail.

- **You are doing the work of leadership:** Leading is a joy in good times because problems are manageable and cash flow is predictable. In tough times, problems can burst and spring leaks like pipes on a submarine that's exceeded its depth limits. The pressure is intense and stressful, but you are the leader. It's your job to make tough decisions and navigate the company back to safer waters. Do the work of leadership.

- **Communicate openly at all levels of the company:** Those you lead need to hear from you. They seek reassurance from you that the company is on the right course. They need and derive energy from "atta boys" from you. Most of all, you need to invest the time to clearly provide details on what the company is doing and where it's at – even if it's not good news. Information shuts down the rumor mill and eliminates drama.

- **Be the light – not the darkness:** Keep your stress, fears and any thoughts of gloom out of sight. True, you are human and deserve to vent and express yourself. But as leader, the eyes of your company are upon you. The no-compromise leader empowers.

- **Balance is everything:** I work out. It keeps me energized, it keeps me healthy, and it helps me manage the natural stress that comes with leadership. What are you doing?

It's truly inspiring to see leaders confronting the effects of the recession head on and making the tough decisions. Rest assured, the leadership lessons we're all learning in these tough times will create an abundance of no-compromise leaders at the other side of this recession.

The no-compromise leader
in you
must prevail.

What are your department managers really doing?

Things may appear to be chugging along just fine. Your managers are not only busy, they may even tell you how little time they have. The numbers are telling a different story. Productivity rates are flat. Work schedules are out of synch with client demand. Performance reviews are off schedule. And there's a developing pattern of missing sales goals.

Sound familiar? If so, what you're experiencing is "free-floating leadership." It's when communication, information flow, follow-through and accountability become cumbersome and slow. It's when discussions are held, solutions or tasks are agreed upon, the meeting adjourns – and nothing happens.

This scenario plays out in business all day, every day. It's a costly and highly inefficient affliction that plagues many leaders. Most importantly, this behavior emanates from the very top, from you.

- **Clarify expectations:** What outcomes are you looking for? Make them high-definition clear. Ask your managers follow-up questions to be sure the outcomes are understood.

- **Crank up information flow:** Energy from monthly or weekly leadership meetings evaporates in an instant. Daily briefings keep everyone focused. Better to know someone is stuck today than on the day before the project is due.

- **Seek ownership of critical numbers and projects:** Never agree to a solution, project or task without assigning someone to own it, what critical numbers will measure success, and what the completion date is.

- **The action is where staff and clients are:** Are your managers afflicted with "office-itis"? Performance is assured and money is made when managers take time to work with staff and clients – not sitting in an office.

- **Work on the right stuff:** It's so easy to get lost working on the small stuff. I equate this to spending all day pushing a grain of sand around your desk. You're busy and working hard on something totally insignificant.

- **Plan to deliver big results:** Isolate and target the big stuff – those projects and tasks that will push growth faster and more efficiently. Get buy-in and commitment from the leadership team. Track the action. Keep score. The clock is ticking. Tick tock. Tick tock. Tick tock. 🖐

Never agree to a solution, project or task without assigning **someone to own it.**

Employee challenges: When do they end?

While discussing leadership responses to employee challenges at a Strategies seminar, a business owner asked, "When does it end?" The entire room could feel the frustration and anguish in her voice. "It's like a battle," she continued. "You nurture, coach, inspire and discipline, and just when you think you've got everyone on the same page – it starts all over again. Doesn't it ever end?" These statements were not coming from a naive business owner. She clearly understood that the answer to her question was: "No, it doesn't end."

Employee challenges can wear you down. From behavioral issues and performance problems to simply following the policies and procedures of the company, leading people can be like a game of "what are they going to throw at me next?" Likewise, leadership can be an incredible journey of discovery of your own ability to grow a company by harnessing and orchestrating the abilities of those you lead. Only you can decide the route of your leadership journey.

- **Embrace your role as a leader:** Yes, the nonsense and craziness of leading people is all part of the experience. It's not going to go away. You can't hide from it or ignore it. Leaders engage. And like a shepherd, leaders continuously tend their flock.

- **Relentlessly communicate:** It never fails. When leaders back off on communication and information flow, the wrong stuff happens. Leaders set the tone, pace and performance of a company – this doesn't happen on its own. There is no "autopilot" setting in your role as leader. If you want more of the right stuff to happen, you must communicate.

- **Know your strengths:** You excel at some aspects of leadership and struggle with others. That's why the best leadership teams are a mixture of skills and abilities. Surround yourself with others who fill your leadership gaps. This isn't an excuse, however, not to further your abilities through training and coaching. Getting better is still the name of the game.

- **Never confuse coaching with confrontation:** I've met too many leaders who crumble when it comes to addressing an individual's behavior or performance issues. "I hate confrontation" is a dangerous statement for a leader to make. Leaders should coach with the intent to help others achieve their full potential. If every coaching opportunity is viewed as a "confrontation," your leadership journey will be a struggle.

- **Know when to cut people loose:** Allowing toxic employees to remain in the company is pure leadership compromise. Do yourself, your team and your company a favor and cut them loose.

- **Maintain your perspective:** It is impossible to be in a leadership role without experiencing stress. It's how you respond to stress that really matters. More often than not, stress is amplified when tough decisions are delayed or even worse, avoided. Again, leaders need to engage. Tackle tough issues in a timely matter. That's the very best way to get back to having fun. 🐄

When leaders back off on **communication and information flow,** the wrong stuff happens.

Don't wait too long to fire someone

I'm asked this question more times than I care to remember. It usually surfaces when a leader's frustration with an employee's performance and/or behavior has been tolerated far too long. The question often means that the leader has been avoiding a difficult conversation or tough decision at the expense of the company and its culture.

The firing of an employee should never be taken lightly. Leaders must accept a high degree of ownership in the failure of an employee to perform up to expectations. When a leader observes subpar performance and avoids engaging in open, honest and direct conversation with the employee, the situation becomes more toxic. And, as stress levels rise, the leader's attention is diverted away from the work that really matters.

I refer to such situations as "intolerable toleration." You don't like what you're seeing and you're not doing anything to fix it. If the question of how long do you wait until you fire someone has been banging around your head, I offer these no-compromise insights:

- **Is it long past "career opportunity" time?** You coached, fired countless warning shots, had the conversations, threatened demotion or termination – and the problems persist. Yes, it's time to offer this employee a career opportunity to work somewhere else. It is long past time.

- **Are you stuck in the employee's stuff?** It is so easy to get sucked into and wrapped up in an employee's personal situations, issues and problems. I am all for helping, encouraging, supporting and showing loyalty to individuals who get derailed by personal stuff. But there is a point when noticeable progress should be seen. That point is when you are fighting harder to protect the employee's paycheck than the employee. Maintain your objectivity or you will get sucked in. You have a company to run and these are tough times. Snap out of it.

- **Are you an "I want to be liked by all" leader?** If you are on a quest to be the most successful "good guy" leader of all time, you need a new mantra. Try this one: "I want to be respected by all." Leadership is more about courage, tenacity and integrity than being well-liked. It takes a lot of discipline to move an entire company forward. Some of that discipline involves tough decisions that fall outside your comfort zone, such as firing problem employees. If you do the work of leadership, you will earn respect. You may even be liked by most – but not all.

- **Are you hanging on to the employee for the wrong reason?** "But this employee brings in a lot of money." When a leader turns his or back on a host of unacceptable behaviors just to hang on to that employee's one big attribute, it is a compromise with far-reaching implications. Sure, you can hang on to the sales or whatever this employee excels at, but what does this do to your company culture? How do your other team members see and respond to this? Double standards are toxic and feed the "why should I care" thinking that wrecks cultures. Whatever you think you're benefiting by holding on to such an employee is costing you 10 times that in drama and putting out fires. Yes, it's time to fire your superstar. 🐓

By the time you ask,
**"How long do you wait
until you fire some one?",**
you've already waited
too long.

The importance of emptying your bucket

A business owner and long-time Strategies customer called to share her voyage during the past few years. She told me about how toxic her company's culture was and that no matter how she tried to fix it, it just got worse. She told me about the painful exodus of key staff and how that left her feeling ineffective as a leader – and resentful. She worked hard on systems and structure; she just couldn't figure out why these setbacks kept happening.

What was once a determined and driven leader now felt defeated, her confidence lost, her energy gone. She fell into a state of depression and out of love with her company. So much so that she began sending out resumes and even went on a number of interviews at some prominent companies. What she discovered during those interviews was a turning point. "These companies were worse than mine," she said. "People forgot about the interviews. There was rude reception staff and phones ringing that no one seemed to hear. Why would I want to work in these places under this kind of leadership?"

"I felt like I hit bottom," she admitted, "and it was time to climb out of this funk." The first thing she did was take ownership of her situation and the state of her business. The next thing she did was acknowledge her communication skills were horrendous. "I was short with people. Although I thought I was clarifying my expectations, I wasn't, and that frustrated my team. And I just didn't give praise enough."

Ownership of the situation allowed this leader to commit to revamping how she communicates. And this is where the breakthrough occurred. She explained how in the past each week would end with a bucketful of conversations that she avoided. The stress of that overflowing bucket is what drove employees out the door and her into depression. She figured out how to have the right conversations when they needed to be done.

I could hear the pride in her voice when she said, "I never end my week with conversations waiting in my bucket – and I feel great." Even the haphazard performance reviews are back on schedule. They begin with the leader giving praise for some aspect of the employee's work, followed by the employee giving praise for something the leader did. From there, the conversations are open and respectful, and nothing is left unsaid.

Do not underestimate the importance of this. It's the conversations that accumulate in your bucket that do the most damage to your company's ability to perform at its best. Avoiding a conversation today only means a more stressful conversation tomorrow. Not clarifying your expectations always results in wasted time, resources and stress. Engaging as a leader to ensure the integrity, performance and security of the company is your responsibility. Allowing your personal leadership blockages, procrastination and avoidance behaviors to get in the way can and will result in stress, frustration and turnover.

Empty your bucket at least once per week. You will find your leadership life lighter and more effective. Your employees will appreciate knowing where they stand and what your expectations are. Communication. It's a bigger deal than you think. 🖐

Allowing your personal
leadership blockages
to get in the way
can and will result in
stress, frustration
and turnover.

How to get more done in less time

Surprise! There just aren't enough hours in the day to accomplish everything that needs to get done. But you already knew that. Like virtually everyone in business today, you begin each day jammed-packed with stuff that needs to get done – then find yourself bombarded with new stuff all labeled "urgent." Checking and responding to the e-mails that accumulated overnight takes an immediate bite of your day. Then come the phone calls, meetings, interruptions, questions and cries for help. Of course, we can't forget time spent consoling that one employee who meanders from one life crisis to the next. Isn't it amazing how something like breaking up with a boyfriend can bring an entire department's productivity to a grinding halt? At the end of the day, your to-do list not only looks the same, it got bigger. If I captured a day in your life, read on.

I always like to use the phrase, "manage what's on your plate" as a means of avoiding the stress that comes from living in a perpetual state of feeling overwhelmed. That's easier said than done. Overcoming bad work habits, poor time management and the inability to quickly filter out priorities, gotta-do items and hot opportunities from the busy work, and nice-to-do tasks, requires more than good intentions.

- **Step off the merry-go-round:** Give yourself the some time to gain perspective on what needs to change in your daily approach to work. You can't do this while you're immersed in your self-inflicted chaos. This may require a few hours or a few days of self-discovery. It all depends on how chaotic your days are. If you're not getting stuff done, stepping back for a bit to reorganize is the key to getting more productive.

- **Filtering and processing your plates:** It's so easy to have projects and problems creep onto your plate. So why not think in terms of two plates? There's your main-course plate that contains high-value, high-priority projects and tasks. Nothing gets added to this plate if it doesn't fit the high-value, high-priority criteria. The second plate is dessert with low-value, low-priority projects and tasks. Like dessert, you may not always have room or you just may pass on it entirely. Finishing what's on the main plate is non-negotiable. Dessert can wait.

- **Organize and prioritize tomorrow's work:** The brain does amazing work while you sleep – as long as you give it stuff to work on. If you organize and prioritize your plates at the end of the day, your brain essentially begins working on tomorrow's tasks. The next day, this subliminal head-start gets you into a productivity mode quickly. The key is working your plan. Yes, interruptions will occur, and it's your job to filter them into high or low priority to avoid heading off on rabbit trails.

- **Assess your progress:** At the end of the day, your reward for getting organized and focused is being able to assess what you've accomplished. View this step as your commitment to personal accountability. Your goal is to achieve measureable progress at the end of every day.

Sure, there will be days you'll find yourself back on the merry-go-round. It happens to the best leaders. No-compromise leaders regain focus and quickly shift back into productivity mode. ✒

Finishing
what's on the main plate
is non-negotiable.
Dessert can wait.

Feed on solutions not problems

Leaders deal with problems every day, all day. It's your job. Big, small and in between, problems will seek you out like metal to a magnet. Here's the good news: You have a choice as to how to deal with them. You can let them get the best of you, or you can accept them for what they are – unplanned occurrences that require correction. When you let them get the best of you, they will almost always take you and your company off course by injecting drama, conflict, excuses, blame, hurt feelings and even witch hunts to find a fall guy to pin the problem on.

It's amazing how people can spin any size problem into a black hole that sucks players and bystanders into its vortex. People seem to feed on the problem, giving it more and more energy as it spins further out of control. Endless debate ensues. Indecision becomes the norm. Leaders stress. Managers shut down. Employees become indifferent. Productivity suffers. Customers defect. Everyone loses.

Now, what would it look like if you and your company fed on finding solutions for unplanned occurrences?

- **Classify it:** What kind of problem are you dealing with? Is it a low-level problem with a straightforward solution? If so, keep it low level. If it's a big problem, pull in the people and resources to contain it and fix it. Objectivity must rule. Keep emotions out of it. Emotions distort the level and magnitude of a problem.

- **And then there are the dreaded dilemmas:** A dilemma has no clear solution and forces innovation. Treat a problem as a dilemma and it will become a dilemma. Solving a dilemma almost always forces innovation and breakthroughs. Feed on identifying solutions that may work. Avoid endless debates over what won't work. Feed innovative thinking by listing the most outrageous solutions because that's where the breakthroughs may be waiting to be discovered.

- **It's not about you:** The worst thing a leader can do is filter solutions based on his or her own leadership blockages. Take three or four steps out of your comfort zone and objectively process the solutions. You may have to make an unpopular decision. Make it. You may have to have that conversation you've been avoiding. Have it. Think about all the problems that became bigger simply because you hesitated, procrastinated and/or obsessed over something that you knew was the right thing to do.

- **Tight deadlines rock:** Give people a lot of time to find a solution and they'll take a lot of time finding a solution. And they'll probably find it right at the eleventh hour anyway. Tight deadlines create a sense of urgency and fuel innovation. Very often, it's seemingly impossible deadlines that yield the greatest breakthroughs. Assigning account-ability for finding a solution without a deadline is an open invitation for problems to multiply out of control.

It's amazing how people can **spin any size problem** into a black hole that sucks players and bystanders into its vortex.

- **Squirt gun vs. fire hose:** This is a tough one that all leaders wrestle with. Can the problem be fixed with a squirt gun or does it need a high-pressure fire hose? True, there are times when reaching for the fire hose may seem like overkill, but most recurring problems happen because the squirt gun and its sugar water were nothing more than a quick fix. Problems tend to have multiple layers that squirt guns do little to reveal, let alone fix. Sometimes it takes a blast from the fire hose to see and wash away all of the underlying causes – and grab everyone's attention. There will be times when you blast a problem with your fire hose by mistake. No-compromise leaders handle such errors with respect and apology – and a towel.

Feeding on solutions is the no-compromise approach. Feeding on problems just pulls you and everyone else deeper in the vortex of drama and lost opportunities. 🐾

When the most significant breakthroughs occur

I've been doing Strategies' Incubator seminars for almost 20 years and still find them to be the perfect blend of grueling and fulfilling. "Grueling" because the intent of Incubator is to break through the barriers of "status quo" and fear of change – to challenge the limitations of traditional business thinking and behavior. "Fulfilling" because helping others achieve their own breakthroughs to new and extraordinary possibilities is an honor and a privilege that I respect and cherish. It doesn't matter if you're the guide or the traveler, achieving breakthroughs takes courage, patience and the determination to not only begin the voyage – but to reach the destinations you set out to achieve.

The most gratifying part of leading an Incubator is to see the light bulbs turning on as people start to shift their thinking and envision the possibilities. The only challenge is to keep the fear of change in proper perspective. As long as the leader can stay committed to the change process, the breakthroughs will come. Employees will rise to the occasion. All breakthroughs are preceded by change.

- **The trigger:** When status quo becomes unacceptable – when the need for innovation and change reaches a fevered pitch – it triggers leaders into action. It can simply be that point where "enough is enough." The key is for leaders to recognize the triggers that initiate the quest for breakthroughs. Ignore the triggers, and the business and everyone associated with it remain stuck in a state of mediocrity – or something worse.

- **The destination:** Once the breakthrough trigger is fired, leaders need to decide on a destination. It's like sticking a pin on a globe that communicates to everyone, "This is where we are going." The destination needs to be big. It needs to pull you and every member of your team toward it. It must make you and your business stretch because significant breakthroughs just don't exist at the low rungs of the ladder.

- **The critical first 15 percent:** Once your destination is identified, it is that initial 15 percent of energy, creativity and crafting your plan that will get you 85 percent of the results. That first 15 percent requires tremendous effort and concentration because it establishes the strategy to reach that destination. Consider the first 15 percent all of the prep work necessary to begin a voyage. If you just give it five percent – you'll be starting your voyage unprepared and putting everyone at risk.

- **Your unique path:** Breakthroughs are one of a kind. Your breakthrough is going to be special to you and your business. You will experiment. You will have successes and gain ground. You will have failures and lose ground. There is no map for you to follow because breakthroughs reside on the other side of the unknown. If you keep waiting for someone to hand you a map, nothing will change.

- **Starts and stops vs. driving forward and regrouping:** Driving forward and taking time to regroup is essential to achieving breakthroughs. Regrouping is like a rest stop where you catch your breath, assess what lies ahead and replenish your fuel before pressing forward. It's the unplanned starts and stops that can wear you down and jeopardize achieving breakthroughs. You stop under pressure, self-doubt and fear. Getting started again means you must now re-convince yourself that you can do it. And while you're trying to convince yourself to get back in the game, your team already interprets the stop as giving up – another broken promise.

- **Beware of straight roads:** The road to a breakthrough is full of twists and turns. Some of it may be straight and paved while other parts are dirt trails. The danger of being on a straight road for extended periods is that you get comfortable and put down your guard. Consider every straight road as nothing more than the opportunity to gain ground while being vigilant to potential hazards. You can lose control and crash simply because you're not paying attention.

- **Savor the wins:** Take time to celebrate progress. Little wins are motivating for you and your team. 🐓

Everyone is responsible for business growth

One of my favorite Neilisms is, "If I can't sleep at night, no one sleeps at night." It's a thought-provoking and rather amusing quote to drive home the fact that leaders don't have to shoulder the burden of growing a business alone. Leaders define the destination and keep the business on a steady course. That's the real work of leadership and includes inspiring great performance as well as making tough decisions.

Leadership is a delicate concoction of foresight, focus, tenacity, trust building and accountability that produces measureable results. When this concoction gets out of whack, those results can head in the wrong direction, signaling that indifference has contaminated the business culture. Indifference is another word for apathy, and apathy can kill a business.

When the funk of apathy slows down a business, leaders typically identify employees as the problem. They reason that employees just don't get it or care, or that they're simply lazy. Well, my fearless leader, I bet you know where this is going. Bingo! It's not them. You're enabling the very behavior that's slowing down your business by not engaging as the leader.

Everyone is responsible for business growth. It's such a basic statement that resonates with good stuff like teamwork, empowerment and progress. But that "everyone is responsible" thinking begins with the leader creating a culture where clarity, openness, trust and shared accountability are the rule rather than the exception. In such a culture, the only way indifference and apathy can set in is when the leader is distracted or just not paying attention.

Sense of urgency is a key business driver. It's the business equivalent of a throttle on a jet. Take the pressure off for only a second and it begins a steady decent. If you're dealing with lackluster performance, indifference and apathy in your business, if you want everyone to be responsible for business growth, then it's time to take the pilot's seat, push forward on the throttle and communicate to your team what the destination is and what it's going to take to get there. That's what no-compromise leaders do. 🐔

*Do as I say,
not as I do.*

Are you keeping your promise to the customer?

These days, terms like "brand promise," "exceeding customer expectations" and "the customer is always right" are so overused that their message is barely audible above the daily activities and routines at your business. Of course you and your team know how essential it is to deliver amazing customer experiences all day, every day. In fact, strategically placed at the core of your business thinking, there is a promise you've made to your customer. That promise is something that only your business can deliver. That promise says your business is committed to delivering the extreme value with extraordinary consistency. It doesn't really matter what your price point is or what segment of the market you cater to, it just matters that you deliver on your promise to the customer to be your best.

The question I pose to you is simple: Is your business keeping its promise to your customers? It's a "yes" or "no" answer. An answer like, "Most of the time," is unacceptable because it's a compromise to your promise. Actually, the reality at your business may be that some people believe in and deliver on the promise – the rest of your team delivers something less. That's breaking your promise. That's compromise.

1. **You need to commit first:** If your business has compromised on its promise, as the leader, you watched it happen. It will take a major initiative and a lot of pushing to get your entire team up to speed. You must be resolute.

2. **Define your promise:** Create a two- or three-person team charged with the responsibility to define every aspect of your promise. What does it look like, feel like and sound like from a customer perspective?

3. **Skill certify everyone:** Build skill-certification training modules that address phone skills, greetings, consultations, client interaction, service-closing procedures, client-assistance procedures, problem

procedures, ending-the-visit procedures – you name it, train and skill certify everyone how to do it all perfectly.

4. **Across-the-board accountability:** This is where no-compromise leadership needs to engage and stay engaged. It's keeping the promise 100% – or it's compromise.

All too often, customers are at the receiving end of a company's indifference and apathy. And sadly, too many customers have gotten used to inconsistent service and the breaching of a company's promise to deliver amazing experiences. The winners invest the time and energy to master the disciplines of customer service and respect. By doing so, the no-compromise winners stand out like shining stars in a sea of mediocrity. Can you deliver on your promise?

If your business
**has compromised
on its promise,**
as the leader,
you watched
it happen.

Simple systems drive customer loyalty

A quick Neilism: "Systems set leaders free." If you want consistency in customer service, satisfaction and retention, you must use systems. A football coach has his playbook – a collection of systems designed to produce specific results. What does your company's playbook look like?

Customers are on the receiving end of your systems. If those systems are designed well and your team follows those systems with discipline and resolve, you have the best chance of achieving consistent and pre-dictable results. If you're lacking systems, or they're poorly design and not adhered to, your customers are on the receiving end of compromise. Your company phone won't be answered correctly. Customers will be on hold too long. Problems will take longer to resolve. Retention will suffer.

Simple or complex, customer-loyalty systems just make work move more smoothly. I stopped at a diner for breakfast with a client. It was one of those popular local spots with lots of character. The waitress would come by and pour some decaf for my client and some high-test for me. She had a lot of tables to take care of and I began to wonder how she could remember who had decaf or regular. I decided to ask. "It's simple," she said, "the decaf cups have two red rings around the top and the cups for regular have one black ring." Duh. What a simple and efficient system.

- **Go critical.** Begin identifying the critical areas in your business that have the greatest impact (positive and negative) on customer loyalty. Prioritize this list and assign teams to design, test and implement the new systems.

- **Set time standards for all points of contact with customers including:** answering calls within three rings, greeting and acknowledging customers with thirty seconds, never leaving a customer on hold for more than two minutes, etc.

- **Connect the dots.** Tie your critical number for customer loyalty, specifically your first-time retention rate, as one of the qualifiers for a bonus payout. This sends a clear message to employees that if the company can't maintain satisfactory retention rates, it can't afford to pay bonus. Strategies has a coaching client who bases 50 percent of the bonus payout on his company's ability to maintain a first-time retention rate of 50 percent or better. He's been working this for more than a year and his first-time retention has never dropped below 54 percent.

- **Collect key data.** Are you collecting data on customer preferences, order history, birth date, favorite sport, or any other information that can help your company tailor each customer's experience? What are your systems for collecting this data and getting it into a central database for service providers, your sales team and customer-service representatives to access? If you allow client data to reside in the memory cells of your service providers, don't complain when clients follow them when they leave. To build a company relationship with clients, you've got to work at it.

Customers are
on the receiving end
of your systems.

- **Deal with customer problems.** What's your system to ensure that problems, even the smallest concerns, are documented and reported so follow-up actions can be initiated? What's the paper or document trail? Who follows up with the customer? When? How?

- **Identify and fill customer needs.** Is there a system for your sales or customer-service staff to follow to design the best solutions? That last thing you want in your business is an "order taker." Taking an order is ordinary. Customizing a prescribed service and product regimen to truly satisfy a customer's needs is extraordinary.

What's your hang time?

You knew it was time to change some things in your business. In fact, you've known this for quite some time. You researched and studied until you felt confident of exactly what you needed to do. You laid out your plan, engaged your leadership team, and hit the launch button to roll out the new program. Your most loyal employees, those who truly believe in your vision, get right to work adapting to the program. They need occasional guidance, support and encouragement, but they're engaged and making progress. You're feeling pretty good.

With every change initiative come change resisters. From the moment you hit that launch button, they start popping up. You know they're productive and otherwise loyal employees; they just seem to have difficulty adapting to new procedures, systems and business designs. You keep pressing forward even while fighting fires caused by those change resisters. It's not that they are openly trying to mutiny, far from it. They're just not playing, and you're concerned that if you start pushing hard on accountability, you'll only make matters worse by creating more tension.

At about 90 days into your change initiative, you realize that the initiative actually died in the first 30 days. Once again, your hang time on leading a new program is short. You know it. Your employees know it. And, make no mistake; your customers even know it.

So what causes projects and initiatives – no matter how small – to crash and burn? The answer is simple: Hang time is all about leadership – your leadership.

- **Employees don't kill change initiatives on their own.** Leaders allow it to happen. They even watch it happen. Leadership blockages such as a fear of confrontation, feeling intimidated, reluctance to make tough decisions, self-esteem issues and other emotional challenges, cause leaders to give in to even the slightest resistance.

- **Fuzzy visions and objectives kill change initiatives.** "OK team, we're gonna move that mountain over there right now. Let's do it." "Why are we moving that mountain? Exactly where are we moving the mountain?

We don't know how to move a mountain. Will we be trained? How long do we have to move it? What resources can we use? This is a big project. How will we be kept informed of our progress?" Crystal-clear visions and well-defined expectations from the outset are the foundation that all change is built on.

- **Mediocrity and indifference kill change initiatives.** A non-negotiable companion of change is accountability. First, leaders must hold themselves accountable to see the initiative through to success. Second, leaders must hold their team members accountable – that means all team members. There is no room for favorites or "get-out-of-jail-free cards" for anyone. Yes, fairness and compassion must prevail, but not at the expense of derailing the initiative. Third, there comes a time when change resisters must be given career opportunities out in the job market.

Crystal-clear visions and well-defined expectations from the outset are the foundation that all change is built on.

- **Stifle innovation, creativity and collaboration, and you kill change.** Any new project, system or change initiative will gain lift and momentum when team members are allowed to shape and tweak it. Involvement spurs ownership thinking and pride. Collaboration spurs unity and strengthening of the company culture, requiring less energy and fewer resources. However, it is the leader's responsibility to ensure that the initiative stays true to its objective and timeline.

If your business suffers from short hang times on new projects and initiatives, ask yourself why. "They" are not sabotaging your success – it's you, your style of leadership and accountabilities you're avoiding or ignoring. What will your hang time be on changing you? 🐓

Decide to take your business to the next level

Here's one of my favorite questions to ask seminar audiences: "How many here want to take their business to the next level?" As if shot from cannons, hands reach to the heavens. Since this "next level" must be a pretty special place, I ask people to describe it. Interestingly, when put on the spot, most answers are vague. Descriptions sound like, "to be profitable, expand, market dominance, brand recognition, debt free, and financial freedom." I like to tease and say, "So you're not really sure. It just has to be better than where you are at now." Everyone uncomfortably chuckles in agreement.

Like a minor league baseball player getting tapped to play in the majors, what if I granted your wish and lifted your business to that next level? Instantly, you would find yourself leading a much more complicated and sophisticated business entity. The pace is fast and relentless. Accountability is intense. Your schedule is jammed. Decisions are huge with far-reaching implications. Reports are piled high. You're trying to figure out how to get a "sense of urgency" to spread beyond your office door. Financial systems and cash-flow pressures have you yearning for simpler days at the level below. Your wish came true. You're in the big game now. You feel as though you entered the Twilight Zone.

Imagine how a baseball player feels being sent back to the minor leagues. The message is simple; he didn't have what it takes to play in the majors. Now, imagine how you would feel if I told you, "We need to have a serious conversation. I granted your wish to get your business to the next level – and you're in over your head. I'm sending you and your business back." For most this would be a tremendous blow in every conceivable sense. For some it would be a relief.

Are you ready to lead your business at the next level? Considering your current leadership style, accountability to get things done, ability to communicate effectively across multi-layers of management, and financial literacy, are you truly ready? Chances are, how you lead today will require a major upgrade to lead at the next level – and to avoid getting sent back to the minors. In business, the sobering reality is that going back to the minors usually means sustaining massive financial losses. Sometimes, losing everything you spent your life building. I mean everything.

I hope this serves as a true wake-up call to assess and upgrade your current leadership abilities. Don't make the fatal mistake many others have made and attempt to lead a next-level company with minor-league leadership skills. In fact, you'll never make it to the next level if you don't upgrade now – start leading like a next-level leader now.

The next level is waiting for you. Don't let your competition get there first. 🕊

Chances are,
how you lead today
will require a major upgrade
to lead at the next level –
and to avoid
getting sent back
to the minors.

Why current reality is never good enough

I often wish I could have my coaching clients lie on a couch while I sit in a big leather chair asking deep questions and taking notes. I'm not a psychologist nor do I want to be one. But just as a psychologist's job is to help patients seek understanding and clarity, my job is to help leaders navigate the unpredictable waters of leadership, business, finance and human dynamics.

In many ways, it's the leader's job to fret over darn near everything. It's the leader's job to constantly move the company forward. If the company is stuck or in the fiery pits of hell, it's the leader's job to unstick it and get the company on the path to daylight. When the company hits goal or has any sort of big win, it's only a short respite to celebrate, and then it's back to the game of business.

Current reality can never be good enough when you're a leader. A problem needs to be solved because another problem is on the way. Today's innovation will become tomorrow's commodity. A win needs to be followed by another win. The relentless pace of change recognizes current reality as imperfect. That makes current reality every leader's nemesis. It's pretty exhausting when you think about it.

- **Imperfect but good:** When your job is to obsess over everything, it's easy to see all the things that are wrong and need fixing. It's easy to get stuck in the "nothing is good enough" mode. Well, buck up. Everything isn't wrong, broken or not working. You and your business had to do a whole lot of things right to get where you are - even if where you are isn't such a fun place right now. So, before you beat yourself and your company up for what you don't like, take time to appreciate all that's good and wonderful about your company. You deserve it. Your team deserves it. Lighten up for a bit.

- **Friend not foe:** One of my current realities is that I cannot consistently ride my favorite 30-mile bike route at a speed of more than 17 miles-per-hour. There are a fair number of hills and I'm just not a fast hill climber. But I keep trying. My current reality is simply a benchmark, something to improve upon. Shift that thinking to business and leadership, and current reality will start working to your advantage.

- **Own don't blame:** Don't like your company's current reality? Well, you led it there. When you engage in the blame, justify, and defend game, your current reality is going to become more imperfect, stressful and intolerable. More things will go wrong and spiral out of control. The first step to improve current reality is for the leader who led it there to own it. And I mean own it all.

- **Encouragement not discouragement:** When you allow your current reality to wear you down and get the best of you, it will have a discouraging effect on not only you but on your entire team. Employees will pick up on your funk and become depressed right along with you. If you position current reality as a benchmark, you can tap into its motivational aspects, just as I do with my bike riding. Try: "Let's get better; let's be the best" to lift and improve team performance.

The relentless pace of change
recognizes current reality as imperfect.

- **Action not inaction:** You change your current reality by taking positive action. Inaction will just give you more of what you don't want. So, look for the possibilities. Or, you can continue to look down at current reality and lead your company right over the cliff you would have seen if you were paying attention. 🐔

Neilism:
Financial reports are a numeric readout
of your company's thinking and behavior.

Numbers

How hard are you playing the game of business?

Here are the facts: Business is a game. You play to win. There are owners, managers, coaches and players. The "season" is 12 months – one game per month. You have the option to draft young, talented players for your team or hire experienced free agents. Competitive teams are always attempting to recruit your best players. You have game strategies and action plans. Customers are your fans. Some fans are fiercely loyal and will stick with your business in good times and bad. Other fans will shift their loyalty to another team should you disappoint. Financial reports are the scorecards.

To have a winning season, your Profit-and-Loss Statement scorecard must show a profit that is equal to or better than what you projected. Your Balance Sheet scorecard must show that your business is healthy. Your Statement of Cash Flows scorecard must show sufficient cash reserves to fund growth and ensure that the business can weather a severe financial storm.

Yes, business is a game, a very serious game. Careers, livelihoods, family security, retirement and more all rely on you and your abilities to lead your business to win. There's nothing like winning. Winning lights everyone up. Winning makes you feel and act strong. Winning fuels a sense of urgency and keeps your business on the offensive rather than on the defensive.

But then there is that darn thing called "reality." Reality says, "You're not going to win every game. And should you have an undefeated season, cherish it because repeats are few and far between." Reality's best advice is: "Be prepared and expect the unexpected." Reality gives very good advice.

I know what it's like to win and to lose the business game. Losing sucks. Losing brings you down. Losing changes your demeanor to the point where you cannot hide it from employees, family and others you do business with. Losing too often leads you down that dangerous path to high-risk decisions that rarely, if ever, end up being the elusive "magic pill." I prefer to win and push myself to break free from my comfort zone. Comfort zones are safe, where there is no pressure or urgency to push and stretch. Whenever I spend too much time in my comfort zone, my business and everyone associated with it pays the price.

You cannot win the business game hanging out in your comfort zone. It just doesn't work. And if you already think you're leading and functioning outside of your comfort zone, think again. I bet you have some wins you want or need that are within your reach – but you're playing it safe. You need to dial up the intensity and live by the number-one rule of No-Compromise Leadership: "If it needs to be done – get it done."

> You cannot win
> **the business game**
> hanging out in
> your comfort zone.
> It just doesn't work.

How awesome would the wins be if you played the business game hard and fast? I bet you'd break through some of the roadblocks you've been fighting. I bet you'd find that additional 20% growth. I bet your team would quickly shift their collective energies to the objectives and away from the internal drama. Here's the really easy part to all this "playing to win the game" stuff – it's your decision. The question is, will you get out of your comfort zone and go for it? 🐓

Living on the financial edge isn't living

Many years ago, I coined a phrase called "owners' nights." (Yeah, it was one of my first Neilisms.) An owner's night occurs around 2:30 in the morning. Urgent thoughts are spinning around your brain – meeting payroll and the rent or mortgage payment; those looming invoices and credit-card balances. You feel as though you're running at high speed, chasing cash flow and getting nowhere. Tossing and turning, you wish the business gods would just save you from this madness.

When you regard surviving a pay period as a major victory, you're in serious survival mode. OK, maybe for your business, it's not payroll; instead it's that big lease you got yourself into – or that big build-out loan – or that huge bailout loan – or that credit-card debt. Maybe it's that you're living a lifestyle that your business can no longer afford to finance. The source of your financial pain doesn't matter; it hurts. It's stressful. It interferes with the joy of life. It keeps you up at night. I know because I've been there.

Being in the training and coaching business, the Strategies team of coaches and I are always up to our eyeballs leading business owners out of the fiery pits of hell. We see the good, the bad and the seriously ugly. In the very worst cases, there are no words to express how it feels to see an owner lose it all in a real-life nightmare.

Here's the good news: Living on the financial edge is a choice. That's right, it's a choice. I'm not suggesting that a business leader wakes up one day and says, "Today I will lead my company into the fiery pits of hell." What I'm saying is that leaders take their businesses down dangerous paths due to failure to plan, emotional and/or impromptu decisions, failure to engage in sound cash-flow management, failure to keep the vision shining bright, failure to keep information flowing to staff, failure to make tough decisions – you get the picture. It's a choice, and you can make the choice to take the path to daylight now – but only if you commit to work through the tough stuff so you can go the distance.

- **Confront your financial reality:** It's one thing to experience an occasional bind. It's another to live in a perpetual cash crisis day in and day out. It's time to pull your head out of the clouds. It's your spending and your business decisions that keep you in a cash crisis.

- **Build a roadmap to daylight:** You're kidding yourself if you think working harder and bringing in more cash will fix the problem. You must get a handle on exactly how big your problem is and isolate those areas that need to be fixed first. To do this you must create a 12-month cash-flow plan that projects potential revenues to strive for and a budget you will live by.

- **Make the tough decisions:** A cash crisis doesn't go away by tiptoeing around the elephant in the room or hoping the law of attraction will bring you prosperity. Get out the meat cleaver and cut expenses that are nice-to-haves – not gotta-haves. And stop looking at a 55% – 65% payroll cost. Do something about it because it's killing your business.

- **Stop dragging yesterday's bad decisions:** Your business can't gain speed dragging yesterday's debt. Your cash-flow plan must have a credit-card and debt-reduction plan built in to methodically pay down debt.

- **Build your "sleep well" account:** This isn't rocket science. Commit to putting at least 5% of total revenues into a cash-reserve account every week. Pay the reserve account first. If you can't put 5% in one week, then put 2% or 3% in – just put something into the account. View your cash-reserve account as a sacred trust that is not to be touched.

I've seen it time and time again. A business that operates in a constant state of insolvency continues to make bad decisions out of desperation from an owner in survival mode. Likewise, a business with cash reserves makes better decisions because they're made from a position of confidence and financial strength.

Financial security starts with your no-compromise commitment to change. Are you ready to do that? 🐓

It's hard to grow dragging yesterday's debt

Debt is easy to accumulate. The simple act of turning on a light creates debt to the power company. When you purchase products to sell or materials and supplies to run your company, an invoice will be heading your way. The moment an employee shows up for work, you owe that employee a paycheck. Anything you purchase without paying cash creates debt. Operating expenses, payroll, payroll taxes and the like represent debt that you should clear up before it accumulates. If you don't, the weight of that debt gets heavy fast. Add the weight of big loan payments, high-interest debt and credit-card debt, and you have all the ingredients to keep your company on the financial brink.

Think of debt as a chunk of lead. A small chunk is easy to carry around all day. Add heavier chunks, and you'll begin to struggle. Add even bigger chunks, and you'll need a cart in order to keep moving. If you keep adding lead to the cart, it will reach a point that is beyond your strength limits. Now it will require all of your attention to begin eliminating chunks of lead until you can get the cart moving again. And while you're busy eliminating that weight, all progress is stalled. This is what debt does to a company.

- **Profit is not cash:** You see profit on the bottom line – but where's the cash? How can this be? Simple, if you're dragging a lot of debt, all of those principal payments take place on the Balance Sheet. Only the interest appears on your Profit-and-Loss Statement. You're cash-starved because cash generated from profit is being sapped by debt. If you don't understand what you just read, you need financial literacy training – and you need it fast.

- **Think before you spend on credit:** Will the purchase add to an already heavy debt load? Are you already dragging more debt weight than your cash flow can handle? If the thought of adding more debt makes you nauseated, make do with what you have. Listen to that little voice in your head because it's usually right.

- **You must have a cash-flow plan:** If you love that GPS in your car because it always guides you to your destination, why don't you love having and/or following a cash-flow plan? Without a cash-flow plan, you're flying financially blind. And flying financially blind explains why you're dragging more debt than you can handle.

- **Losing weight requires discipline and a plan:** All diets work. It's the dieter who cheats and avoids exercise that's the problem. Reducing debt often requires leaders to make tough decisions, change behaviors and even change lifestyles. You either commit 100% to reducing debt or you continue to live in a state of financial stress. 🐾

Think of debt as a chunk of lead.
A small chunk is easy
to carry around all day.
Add heavier chunks,
and you'll begin
to struggle.

Managing pay expectations

One of the most sensitive and emotional challenges of working through challenging times is dealing with the stress associated with managing pay expectations. For leaders, it's confronting the reality that cash flow may not only call for a pay freeze but may demand decisions on payroll reductions.

For employees, it's the stress of not knowing how the recession will impact their paychecks. Will the pay raises occur this year? Will there even be pay reviews? Could pay be reduced? And the biggest worry of all – will I join the ranks of the unemployed?

In difficult times, pay becomes one of those issues capable of creating a low-level funk that interferes with morale and productivity. It can cause bad feelings as questions and concerns about pay fester.

No-compromise leaders step up in these emotional times to build trust. And they do this by managing expectations about pay. They step up and defuse the emotional stress about pay and job security by eliminating as many question marks as possible. The one thing the no-compromise leader doesn't do is avoid these conversations.

Unfortunately, too many owners try to ignore this issue rather than address it head on. As a result, frustration can begin to surface among employees who wonder just how long this battle of driving the company through tough times will rage on without some sign of reward and appreciation.

- **Get it all out in the open:** Stand before your team and tell them where the company is. Reconnect them with the vision and mission they've been fighting so hard for. Express your appreciation. And tell them the truth about pay and raises. It is always the best strategy to get everyone's feelings on the table, because when you don't, speculation, rumors and bad assumptions will infect your culture. Talk openly about how the company is doing and its financial condition. If the company is encountering cash-flow challenges, get all employees involved in the process of innovating new revenue opportunities and cost-cutting measures.

Getting them engaged in protecting the company – and their paychecks – is a more efficient and productive use of brainpower than trying to hide the truth.

- **Uncertainty yields to understanding:** If you need to initiate a pay freeze, deliver this news yourself and be clear so everyone understands why you made this decision. If you need to lay people off, this too must be done with extreme clarity. Employees will support what they understand – even if the news is not what they want to hear.

No-compromise leaders step up in these critically emotional times **to build trust.**

- **Find other ways to reward:** When raises are out of the question, there are always other rewards you can offer. Just like soldiers are given time away from the front lines to recuperate, give some comp time to those employees who have earned it. A day off or a chance to leave early is a sign of appreciation that won't break the bank. Sending one or more employees for training is a break from the routine of work, that will also pay dividends for your company. Just giving out some gift cards for dinner, movies or special services is a sign of appreciation. A company picnic or barbecue brings staff together. True, these are not raises, but they are rewards that can fill a void.

- **A little goes a long way:** There is always a way to find a little in the budget for those who consistently go above and beyond. A minor "I-wish-I-could-give-you-more" raise is better than nothing. FYI: Take a hard look at some of the stuff you're still spending money on. I'm sure you'll have enough nice-to-haves to cut that will allow well-deserving employees to get some sort of a raise.

- **Define the target:** It is important to define where the company's critical numbers need to be in order to trigger raise opportunities. This places the focus and energy on achieving goals and having wins and away from the "They won't give me a raise" drama that grinds down progress.

- **If you feel it, they feel it:** Avoiding pay conversations is the worst strategy. Doing so is a compromise to the individuals who work to make your company a success. Employees feel the stress and strain of getting a company back on track. Just have the conversations.

- **Be a balanced leader:** You are the keeper of your company vision. And making the necessary tough decisions required in tough times means that you will not please everyone. No-compromise leaders know how to be confident and compassionate.

*Some days you just have
to enjoy the ride.*

How owners make their accountants lazy

I've reviewed thousands of financial statements over my 40 years as a business consultant. I confess that I have become cynical when it comes to accountants. It seems that accountants fall into three groups: those who simply "account" for any info they receive and offer no advice or guidance; those who work diligently to collect, decipher and ensure that the data is correct; and those who truly engage and interact with their clients to help them run financially efficient companies and guide them to prosperous futures.

During my No-Compromise Leadership Vermont Bike Tour, I sat down to chat with long-time fellow speaker Larry Kopsa, a Certified Public Accountant. I've known Larry for many years and have always been impressed with his passion to help entrepreneurs understand their financials and achieve their financial dreams.

Here are Larry's insights about how the thinking and behaviors of entrepreneurs can result in inferior service from their accountants:

- **You get what you pay for:** If you're looking for a cheap accountant, there are plenty. They'll accept whatever information you give them and bang out financial reports and do your tax returns. You'll get nothing more than "garbage in, garbage out." You won't get advice or guidance. You won't get someone who will pay attention to your business. If you want an accountant who will speak in a language you can understand, who will help you create a secure financial future, and who will help you navigate the complex and ever-changing maze of tax laws, then you need to invest in the right accountant and accounting firm. Cheap gets you paperwork. That's all.

- **The infamous drop-off-the-shoebox syndrome:** Too many owners think accountants can read their minds and figure out what all the stuff in the box is. That they can tell if the meal receipt for your company picnic is a 100% deductible expense or a "meals and entertainment" expense that's only a 50% deduction. "Cheap" accountants will just guess what the expense is. Accountants who work to make and save you money will say, "Let's sit down together and figure out what all this stuff is."

- **Not engaging in pre-tax interviews:** Larry meets with clients once or twice per year to review where the business is and what it plans to do. Engaging in one or more pre-tax interviews is the proper way to build a solid plan for the best year-end tax position. Trying to figure it all out at tax time is just too late.

- **Not paying attention to the work the accountant is doing:** Larry writes all over the financial statements that he delivers to clients. He wants the owner to look at them and to pay attention to them. He points out areas of concern and applauds numbers that moved in the right direction. He wants owners to ask questions. When owners receive their financial reports and never ask questions, many accountants assume you don't care, and that can make an accountant "lazy."

The past is just historical data that helps identify problems and opportunities. It's the future that clients and their accountants should be focusing on.

- **Not paying attention to the "Chart of Accounts":** It's so easy to bloat a chart of accounts with a ton of account items until it borders on excessive – like having an account just for coffee rather than grouped under "supplies." Or, having an account for every purchase for each vendor. When Larry starts working with a client, one of the first things he does is clean up the Chart of Accounts so the financial reports make sense and are easier to read.

- **Assuming the accountant truly knows what's going on in your business:** When owners say, "My accountant has that information," it's a symptom of a potential problem. Accountants can't know what's going on in your business just by looking at your numbers. They don't know what you're planning to do. They don't know when your objectives change. They don't know what keeps you up at night unless you tell them. That's why your accountant should ask a lot of questions. That's why you should have regular meetings.

- **Not engaging your accountant as a proactive advisor:** Tax laws are changing. Generating profit is more difficult than ever. Your accountant needs to understand your intentions and where you want to take the business. The "past" is for tax purposes. The past is just historical data that helps identify problems and opportunities. It's the future that clients and their accountants should be focusing on. Have a conversation once a month with your accountant to review financial history and to develop strategies to improve your cash position and ensure that your numbers are within acceptable benchmarks.

- **It's OK to say, "I don't know":** Larry loves it when clients say they don't understand something. He encourages it and wants to make you the most savvy business owner you can be. Again, if you never ask questions or tell your accountant what you don't know, you may be the reason your accountant got lazy.

*Are you forgetting
something?*

The bottom line on growing the top line

The one question every business leader asks is, "What can I do to grow the top line?" It's not just the question that's important; it's the sense of urgency with which it's asked.

A very good customer of Strategies told me that we're great at teaching companies how to build no-compromise cultures, managing cash flow and how to systematize just about everything, but we don't teach how to grow that big nasty top line. During the conversation, he said that we helped him grow his average sales ticket by $15, that his service pre-book ratio has jumped well over 50% and a number of other key ratios are up as well. So, with key ratios up, I'm scratching my head trying to figure out why his top line isn't growing. Something isn't happening. And it's not cranking up social networking or investing in some kind of marketing campaign. It's internal.

- **Hold yourself and every team member accountable:** Here's my mantra for winning in these economic times: If any employee isn't fighting as hard as the company is to make payroll, wake them up or suggest a career opportunity in another company. Stop tolerating mediocrity. If you've been avoiding a straight-talk conversation with one or more employees, you're compromising. If they're not being accountable to your systems, you're the one who's been accepting it rather than addressing it. Afraid someone will quit? Get over it.

- **Rebuild and/or turn your selling systems on:** If you're not getting the results you want, it means your selling systems are incomplete or not being used. Does everyone understand your selling systems? If not, why not? Have you verified that everyone has mastered your systems? If not, why not? Do it.

- **The basics still work better than the new stuff:** Personal contact and interaction is becoming a rare commodity in these days of e-mail and social networking. Pick up the phone and call 25 of your best customers and ask how they're doing. Ask what you can do better. Talk to people. Shake hands with people. How many networking group meetings are you attending each month? If it's less than two, you need to get out more.

- **Show appreciation:** In the daily battle to grow the top line, it's easy to forget the easiest way to grow top line. Just show appreciation for everyone who does business with you and your company. I help and coach people every day. I'm a deeply compassionate individual. However, I realized that I'm guilty of not showing appreciation at the level I can be – and I'm doing something about it. I'm picking up the phone. I'm reconnecting with people I care about and respect who simply fell off my radar.

If any employee isn't fighting as hard as the company is to make payroll, **wake them up** or suggest a career opportunity in another company.

If you're not growing your top line, then you're being too selective about the doing the work that needs to be done. You're avoiding tough decisions. You're placing blame everywhere but where it belongs. 🖎

Neilism:
Do you do quarterly performance
evaluations at least once a year?

Culture

What's lurking behind your company's curtain?

I call it "the curtain," and every company has one. It's that secret place where leaders stash problems, deficiencies, toxic situations, compromising behaviors, poor business practices, spending habits, procrastination and residue from bad decisions. The sole purpose of the curtain is to conceal what's not right with a company from employees, customers, peers, vendors and others. What's behind the curtain is a dark and scary place, a place that saps energy and resources.

While the curtain allows a company to put on its best face by concealing its flaws, sooner or later what's been festering behind the curtain eventually leaks out. When the curtain is breached, the company shifts into damage-control mode. Only decisive leadership action can finally fix what should have been fixed long ago.

- **There's nothing "easy" about stashing stuff behind your curtain:**
  When you take the "stash it behind the curtain" option, what you're stashing never goes away. It just waits while it gets bigger and more complicated. Ask yourself, "Do I want to address this now or deal with a bigger problem tomorrow?" You already know the answer.

- **It's just a curtain – not a bank vault:** Just because it's out of sight, doesn't mean that stuff can't escape or that prying eyes won't find a way to take a peek. Chances are that there's stuff behind your curtain that could hurt the feelings of those who support and believe in you. So, before you stash anything, know that a leak or peek could compromise relationships and break trust. A Neilism: A compromise today becomes a bigger compromise tomorrow.

- **Are you becoming too dependent on your curtain?** When too much stuff accumulates behind your curtain, it signals that "accountability avoidance" has become part of your leadership thinking and behavior. It's a sign that you're heading down a dark and dangerous leadership path where only bad things happen. Acknowledgement of this means that it's time to seek the help and guidance of a mentor, coach or trusted advisor.

- **Throw open your curtain to let the light in and the truth out:** Everyone makes mistakes and decisions that turn out badly. Those around you probably already have an idea of what's behind your curtain. More importantly, your loyal supporters are eager and waiting to step up and help you work through challenges. Keeping stuff behind your curtain is a terrible burden and a tremendous source of stress. Better to have the energy and brainpower of your supporters working on solutions than propping up a burned-out leader.

What's behind the curtain
is a dark and scary place, a place that saps energy and resources.

Step back and examine what's lurking behind your curtain. Fix the small stuff before it becomes big stuff. Confront the big stuff and prove to yourself that you can be the no-compromise leader you deserve to be. And when you're done, have a private ceremony where you throw your curtain into the fire and bid it farewell. ✈

That getting-everyone-on-the-same-page thing

Getting everyone on the same page is what leadership is all about.
So, why is it that leaders often feel that team members are taking plays from the wrong playbook? And why is it that team members often feel that their playbook is missing critical pages, or even worse, wish they were even given a playbook before the game began? Clearly, that getting-everyone-on-the-same-page thing is more complicated and perplexing than most leaders realize.

Here's the downside: When teams are not on the same page, things go wrong. Time, money and resources are wasted. Frustration builds and spreads throughout the team, and everything slows down. Mistakes are made. Quality takes a nosedive. Customer loyalty is compromised. Blame, finger pointing, justification and throwing people under the bus emerge as a new skill set. Yes, we have all lived what I just described – and most of us prefer never to live it again.

Here's the upside: When teams are on the same page, things go right. Time, money and resources are maximized. Morale is high, and work moves along quickly and efficiently. Mistakes rarely occur because everyone is knowledgeable, committed and accountable to the processes, procedures and systems, so much so that innovation perpetuates constant improvement. Best of all, there no more buses around for people to be thrown under.

- **Gotta have a page first:** Stop talking about everyone getting on the same page if you don't have a page for everyone to get on. Too many leaders set up themselves and their teams for failure simply because projects, expectations and outcomes were poorly – or never – defined. Creating the right outcomes and winning in business can only be achieved through a coordinated game plan that everyone understands. So, the next time you say, "We need to get on the same page," I hope someone steps up and asks, "May I have a copy of that page?"

- **Be committed to the process:** Getting everyone on the same page begins at the top. The most frustrating aspect of coaching leaders is their propensity to not play the same game they want everyone else to play. It's impossible to get everyone in a company or department on the same page starting from the middle. That is a guaranteed recipe for frustration, drama and company dysfunction. It must start at the top.

- **Read from the same page every day:** "Hey, let's have a meeting so we can all get on the same page." Just like getting and staying physically fit takes working out and eating well every day, so does getting on the same page. One meeting is nothing more than the locker room speech before the game. Then it's charging out on the field with playbook in hand. It's huddling before every play. It's about execution and achieving excellence. If you can accomplish that in one meeting, I want to write a book about you being the greatest leader in the history of business.

Stop talking about everyone **getting on the same page** if you don't have a page for everyone to get on.

OK, here's the secret sequence to getting everyone on the same page. Vision and desired outcomes first. Mission plan and playbook second. Communicating with absolute clarity third. Daily, weekly and monthly information flow fourth. Accountability and commitment throughout the company is a constant. No compromise rules. 🐔

Is your information flow really a drip?

Right now, this very moment, how many of your employees know exactly what the immediate and most critical objectives are for your business? How many know what needs to be accomplished this month, this week – today? How many clearly understand your expectations for their individual performance? The common denominator for each of these questions is "information flow." With it, there is focus, urgency, efficiency and productivity. Without it, there is frustration, fragmentation and missed opportunities.

We live in an age where information literally flows at the speed of light. Yet, even for those blessed with the latest technology, information flow can be excruciatingly inconsistent. And that means your company ship is springing leaks, taking on water, diverting precious resources and slowing down.

Achieving higher levels of organizational performance always requires a change in the collective behaviors of teams. It doesn't matter if a company is in a crisis situation or striving to reach that really big goal, its ability to disseminate key information will determine how quickly behaviors will change. Too many leaders routinely underestimate the level of information flow that is required for measureable results to occur. And when information drips rather than flows, that quest to reach the next level morphs into a pipedream.

- **Find the bottlenecks:** Every company has them – and you may be one of them. Leaders are notorious for having high expectations and not backing them up with the necessary information to clarify expectations. Are one or more of the team leaders a bottleneck? Are there key players on your team with conflicting agendas? The only way you'll discover the bottlenecks is to spend quality time with your leadership team and employees. If they cannot articulate where the company is going and what its immediate objectives are, there is an information-flow bottleneck.

- **What, why, how, the score:** Everyone needs to know. Everyone needs to play. From daily huddles around the company scoreboard to daily leadership team briefings, the only excuse for not driving information flow is laziness and procrastination. We're in the information age, and we have some amazing technologies to drive it. From conference calls, web-based video meetings and online file sharing, to text messages, e-mails and calendar alerts, there is no excuse for anything less than rapid-fire information flow.

- **Get into the grove and make it stick:** Ratcheting up your information-flow systems requires you to adapt and commit to new disciplines. Don't expect everyone else to commit to an information-flow system that you routinely compromise. The only way to ensure accountability down through the employee ranks is for accountability to be locked in at the top.

> When information drips
> rather than flows,
> the crisis continues
> and that quest to reach
> **the next level morphs
> into a pipedream.**

- **Good systems are no guarantee:** Information flow is not only systems driven, it's behavior- and culture-driven. Add a healthy dose of discipline and accountability to the mix and your systems stand a chance of working. Even in the best conditions, if employees ignore the information that's flowing toward them, systems can fail. Indifference and laziness are the major causes of information-flow inconsistencies and failures. Do you lead with the intent to create and maintain an account-able and disciplined company culture? If not, the leaks will be major. In fact, the water is already past your knees and rising. Engage.

- **Find your information-flow balance:** When it comes to information and data, there is such a thing as too much information. I know I just got you fired up to open the floodgates, but overloading your team with a barrage of information can backfire. First, key information can be lost in the floodwaters. So even though you put the information out there, few team members can find it. Second, flooding your team with information can bog them down with processing information rather than engaging in the work that needs to be done. Translation: Everyone is working really hard; nothing is getting done.

- **Clarity is everything:** When it comes to information flow, short and sweet is not only a beautiful thing, it's the only thing. Think of your information-flow system as a pipeline. That pipeline can only handle so much volume. Trying to push too much volume through can cause it to spring leaks and eventually burst. Leaks are the recurring problems that drive leaders crazy. Leaks can always be traced back to the leader. A burst occurs when leaders jam too much information through their pipeline. A burst always results in some form of a business crisis that requires all hands on deck to contain and fix it. Communicate concisely and with clarity.

Every company needs to monitor their information-flow systems for leaks and inconsistencies. And every company's information-flow systems need to be upgraded and evolve consistently with its growth and current reality. Now, go find your first information-flow leak. You won't have to look very hard. 🐓

*It's not a sign of weakness
to ask for help.*

Passion and heart drive the numbers you want

The numbers of your business measure its performance and efficiency. The numbers measure the collective determination of the team you lead to not only achieve your goals – but to surpass them. The numbers measure your ability to inspire and ignite the passion that exists within every employee. The numbers measure your resolve to lead your company through a crisis. The numbers tell you when you're winning or losing the business game. Yes, the numbers speak volumes about your business and your qualities as a leader.

In the end, though, the numbers are nothing more than numbers. Yet, because business is about money and success, leaders can become all about the numbers. They obsess over scoreboards, daily reports, critical numbers and financial reports. Their words sound like, "We're behind goal. Productivity is down. You didn't make your numbers. Sell more. We're over-budget." The downside of being "all about the numbers" is forgetting that numbers are simply lifeless digits.

In the daily grind of competing in a predatory economy, driving the numbers can override the most potent success factors: passion and heart. Passion and heart drive the numbers. Passion and heart win championships. Passion and heart not only achieve goals; they are the energy that surpasses business goals. If "all about the numbers" has become your leadership mantra, your best intentions may be sapping the life out of those you lead.

- **What is the passion and heart of your business?** You and your employees get out of bed and go to work every day. Why? If it's just to get a paycheck, it's a sure bet that passion and heart are in short supply. I get out of bed every day and go to work to help business leaders survive and thrive in these crazy times. When leaders see nothing but gloom and doom, I help them see and move toward daylight. Does the work of your company serve the greater good? Does it make someone's day? Does it provide solutions? Whatever it is, put it on a pedestal and shine a spotlight on it, so you and every member of your team can see and feel why your business exists.

- **Cheer, celebrate, and awaken your company's passion and heart.** Money may be tight. The bills may be piled high. The funk of missing a goal may have deflated morale. It may even feel as though your employees are plotting a mutiny. If you think announcing that the numbers need to get better and get better fast, is going to ignite the passion to win, snap out of it. What would happen if the equivalent of a marching band playing "Stars and Stripes Forever" paraded through your company? Remember as kid how you could feel that big bass drum beating in your stomach? Wake up your team with an overdose of cheering and celebrating. Throw some popcorn in the microwave. Play with noisemakers. Open the window and let the fresh air in and the gloom and doom out. Have some fun.

If "all about the numbers"
has become
your leadership mantra,
your best intentions
may be sapping the life out of
those you lead.

- **Be with your people.** Smile. Make eye contact. Ask employees how they're doing. Listen to each as if you are the only two people left on earth. Stop being so stingy with your positive reinforcement and say, "Good job." Let them see the real you inside and show them that you care about them, their concerns and their wellbeing.

Rekindle the passion and heart that most certainly does exist in your company. It's there even in the darkest times. If you do, you'll find that even the loftiest goals are within your reach. 🐓

Behaviors first, numbers second

Numbers are used to set targets and measure performance. You use business and industry benchmarks to compare how your business stacks up against the competition. You set goals for service providers and salespeople. You run your financial reports in myriad formats to do a forensic analysis to identify financial leaks and trends that signal trouble or success. Without question, numbers are vital to business. But there's a catch. The numbers you use to guide and analyze your business performance are 100% behavior-driven.

FACT: Behaviors make the numbers that you measure, celebrate and obsess over happen. Given this, why is it that so many leaders bypass the essential role that behaviors play in achieving the numbers they want? Leaders spew out orders like, "You need to get your numbers up," and leaves the conversation believing those numbers are going to change. The problem is that the behaviors that produce the lackluster results are still intact. For the numbers to change, the behaviors need to change first.

From a company financial perspective, I've seen too many leaders build incredible cash-flow plans only to become frustrated that their perfectly formatted profit-and-loss statements and balance sheets are not showing improvement. The gap between the cash-flow plan and achieving the desired profits and value is purely behavior driven. With a system in place that creates and shapes financial disciplines, new and better behaviors will evolve. Financial performance will improve by changing behaviors to control spending and ultimately the management and use of financial resources.

- **Systems shape behaviors:** A system is a series of processes that produces predictable results. Want an individual to produce better numbers? Provide them with the right system and skill development training to make those numbers move in the right direction.

- **Understand the story numbers tell:** Numbers simply tell a story. It's your job to understand the story behind the numbers. What made this number a win? Why is this number causing a problem? If all you do is obsess over the numbers, you'll never undercover the story that contains the lessons behind those numbers.

- **Take responsibility and ownership:** As a leader, all the numbers your business produces happened on your watch. They're your numbers. If they're numbers to celebrate, your leadership inspired the energy and the right environment for those numbers to occur. If those numbers are unacceptable, your leadership played a role in that too. Blame does nothing to change the numbers you don't like. Taking action and making the right decisions is all about behavior. Behavior first, numbers second.

Behaviors make the numbers
that you measure, celebrate
and obsess over happen.

- **Your behavior needs to change first:** Leaders are notorious for double-standard thinking. This means that the behaviors they expect in others aren't necessarily the behaviors that they personally set the standard and example for. If the mandate is to sell more, do more, spend less, and you're doing the opposite, you are the one who is compromising. You are the one who is preventing the numbers that you strive for to occur. No-compromise leadership is about accountability, execution and integrity. 🐔

Entitlement behavior is pure compromise

Double standards communicate that there are entitlement rules and acceptable behaviors for some while others must adhere to more rigid rules. Fact: Double standards compromise the values of a company. Double standards create performance drag. Even the slightest existence of double standards perpetuates entitlement thinking and behavior. And who is the originating source of double standards? You guessed it, the leader – and that means you.

You need to purge entitlement behavior from your company. In extremely embedded cases, the purging may require a total leadership makeover. The problem is that most leaders refuse to acknowledge the problem exists and that they – and their egos – are most likely fueling it.

At the leadership level, entitlement behavior is best described as "do as I say, not as I do" behavior patterns. It's when leaders come in late, fail to follow procedures they themselves established, and generally do what they want – simply because they are the leader.

Entitlement behavior gets critical when leaders begin sapping the company by using the company checkbook as if it were their own. I've seen exotic cars, vacations, mortgage payments, college tuition and home landscaping run through the business. And I've seen trust issues and resentment hurt otherwise great companies when leaders tell employees there's no money for raises, benefits, training and/or upgrading equipment. It doesn't matter if the leader is the owner of the company or not, it is his or her responsibility and duty to protect the integrity of the company – not sap the company at the expense of others.

Leaders further harm their cultures by bestowing entitlement behavior to "favorite" individuals or groups. You know the favorite-employee syndrome is alive and thriving in your company when select employees are held less accountable to the rules, policies and expectations of the company. Examples include overlooking chronic lateness, absenteeism, inappropriate behaviors or sub-standard performance.

This instantly creates a double standard and broadcasts mixed messages to every nook and cranny of the organization. Many are held accountable while some are not. Some get special treatment and privileges while many do not. And then when leaders stand before their teams and speak of vision, values, goals and teamwork, they're frustrated by the apathy and discontent.

You know the
favorite-employee syndrome
is alive and thriving
in your company
when select employees
are held less accountable
to the rules, policies
and expectations
of the company.

Leaders allow entitlement behaviors by failing to engage and correct the behaviors when they surface. Rest assured, every company has its share of employees who continually push and test company rules, policies and procedures. When leaders fail to address these behaviors through one-on-ones, coaching, write-ups or formal reprimands, the behaviors become embedded. There is a direct correlation between the length of time that entitlement behaviors continue and the leadership energy required to correct it. If the leaders lacks the skills to work through these crucial conversations and coaching, the only way to eliminate the behaviors is for them to leave with the employee.

- **Create and model the standards:** You know the basic rules of leadership. You need to change first before you can expect others to follow. Leaders must practice no-compromise behaviors first. Your respect, trust and integrity are on the line. Climb down out of the entitlement clouds.

- **It's time for a culture shift:** Going "no compromise" is non-negotiable. Chart your company's course to an "all for one, one for all" standard. Read my book No-Compromise Leadership. It contains the game plan you need to follow to make the shift in yourself and in your entire business culture.

- **Have the necessary conversations:** You know exactly who on your team is benefiting from the double standards you allow. You must do one-on-ones to clearly define the double standards that are going away and your expectations moving forward. Most of all, you must communicate how you will hold everyone accountable. This is not confrontational – it's leadership fixing what leadership allowed to occur.

> There is a direct correlation between the length of time that **entitlement behaviors continue** and the leadership energy required to correct it.

Keeping a culture is the tough work of leadership. Like keeping weeds out of your garden, it's the type of work that never ends. If entitlement behavior and double standards exist in your company, it's time to start the process of weeding them out – now. Your company will never achieve its true potential and vision dragging such behavior along. 🐓

Trust can only be earned.

When broken commitments compromise trust

If you're in leadership, there is no avoiding the quagmire that results from broken commitments. I'll get the easy part of this discussion out of the way first. As a leader, you must view every commitment you make as a sacred contract. If you promise to return a call before the end of the day – do it. If you commit to a meeting – be there on time and be prepared. If you promise to complete a project – get it done.

Every broken commitment chips away at the level of trust others have in you. If you don't earn and maintain the trust of those you lead, you cannot effectively be their leader. It's that simple.

The more difficult aspect of leadership is the ability to hold others accountable for the tasks, responsibilities and comments they make. Holding others accountable is much of what leadership is all about. It's when leaders fail to hold others accountable that compromise and trust issues surface. The longer the leader allows these issues to continue, the more they chip away at trust – for both the offender and the leader. A leader can lose the trust of employees by allowing others to fail to deliver on even the most basic of commitments.

- **Yes, we love those self-starters:** You cannot expect everyone to possess the "self-starter gene." Many people benefit from leadership environments that help them keep on task. Businesses with high accountability factors are high performers. High-trust factors keep the culture pure. The lower the accountability factor, the more drag, drama, inconsistencies, missed opportunities and trust issues there are.

- **Systems are the foundation of accountability:** Accountability creates urgency and results. Accountability spreads "get it done" thinking throughout a business. The purpose of systems is to create predictable results by eliminating variables. When leaders attempt to be the "accountability system" rather than building systems, they invite frustration and burnout. Acid test: If the performance of your company demands your presence, you are the accountability system. It's time to step back and assess your approach to leadership.

- **Leadership blockages and emotions:** If you have issues holding others accountable to their responsibilities and commitments, if you find such conversations unsettling, I urge you to engage the services of a leadership coach. Working through tough conversations comes with the title of leader. Avoiding such conversations, or attempting to candy-coat your way through them, will cause you to lose the trust of those you lead. (I discuss this in detail in Part One of my *No-Compromise Leadership* book.)

- **Help others restore trust:** Would you rather create a list of consequences for breaking commitments or help others to learn how to be accountable? Procrastination, time management and commitments made with the best intentions exist in every business. Attempting to penalize offenders into submission is a long and dark road. Reach out your hand and become an accountability mentor. Invest the time and resources to help people reach their full potential. If they truly cannot meet the expectations of their position, help them understand that seeking another opportunity is best for all.

A leader can lose
the trust of employees
by allowing others
to fail to deliver
on even the most basic
of commitments.

When 'inner circle' trust is compromised

All leaders have what can be described as an "inner circle" of people who they trust, depend upon and confide in. They are members of their leadership team, advisors, peers and others they do business with. By design, your inner circle is a safe place for you to share confidential information, seek counsel and to vent. Your inner circle is built entirely on trust, respect and confidentiality. That's why you feel comfortable letting your guard down.

As much as it pains me to write this, sooner or later, a member of your inner circle will compromise trust. To think otherwise is naive.

- **Beware the "opportunist":** Have you ever said, "Don't tell anyone, but..."? Of course you have. And chances are that the information you shared in confidence spread like wildfire. Why? Because you just gave an opportunist a big, juicy piece of drama to blab to others. It's nothing more than the "I know something you don't know" game. FACT: Never share highly sensitive information with members of your inner circle who are less than 99% trustworthy. Anything less than 99% and chances are that information will be leaked. That missing 1% is to keep you grounded and make you question if the sensitivity of what you are about to disclose is equal to the trustworthiness of that individual.

- **You still need to trust:** I'd go crazy if I couldn't trust members of my inner circle. I need to share, vent and collaborate openly and freely with my team. That's how I lead and work best. Has my openness backfired on me? Of course it has – at times painfully so. But I regard my openness as a risk worth taking. I've met leaders with trust issues, even with members of their inner circle. In every case, that creates a culture of distrust among those they should trust most. FACT: It's hard to grow a company when the key players are always looking for everyone else's hidden agenda.

- **They have their own inner circles:** So, someone entrusts me by sharing and seeking guidance on a highly sensitive issue. To ensure that I give the best advice, I turn to members of my inner circle where we reach consensus on a solution. Is it possible that members of my inner circle will disclose all or some of the conversation? Yes. Hopefully for the same reason I sought out their input. FACT: When trust and integrity are core values in your culture, sensitive information is respected, and therefore contained, 99% of the time. That 1% is reserved for the opportunist "drama spewer."

Your inner circle is built entirely on **trust, respect and confidentiality.**

- **Yes, it hurts:** When a member of your inner circle compromises trust by lying or sharing private and confidential conversations for personal gain, it hurts – and hurts a lot. You can crawl into your paranoid hole and shut down your trust in all inner circle members. If you take this tack, you just triggered distrust, resentment and hurt feelings in those you should be trusting most. FACT: It's easy to say, "Get over it," but that's exactly what you need to do. Learn from the experience. Grow from it. That's what the no-compromise leader does. 🐦

You need to hear it, and they're afraid to tell you

The usual conversation among leaders is about needed conversations with employees regarding behavior and performance issues. And for those conversations that are guaranteed to raise your blood pressure, there are some fine books available such as *Fierce Conversations* (by Susan Scott) and *Crucial Conversations* (by Kerry Patterson, Joseph Grenny, Ron McMillan and Al Switzler) to help you through. But what happens when employees need to tell you about issues with your behavior your performance as their leader?

This communication blockage is more common than you think. In fact, there's a darn good chance that you have employees in your own company that need to tell you things that you need to need to hear – but can't. Even your most trusted and loyal employees are probably holding back. Why? The answer is summed up in one word: fear. Fear for their jobs. Fear of retribution. Fear that it could send you off on one of your tirades. Fear that your feelings will be hurt.

It is imperative that owners create an environment where open communication on sensitive issues can occur without fear. More importantly, to be an authentic no-compromise leader, you need to be open to constructive feedback from employees. That's how you get better. That's how you mature as a leader and build trust.

- **Leadership team meetings:** Put feedback on your performance on the agenda. Let team members know that you need their feedback in order to be the best leader for them and for the company.

- **Performance reviews:** Make "Where can I improve to support you better?" part of every employee performance review.

- **Cool your jets:** A leader's instant defensive posturing to employee feedback is the most-cited reason employees give to avoid initiating a conversation with their leaders. Rather than going defensive and shutting down the dialogue, acknowledge how much you value the employee's willingness to share feedback with you.

- **Listen:** Don't talk; just listen: Allow the employee to speak. Encourage them to go deeper with statements like, "This is important for me to hear, please explain more."

- **Get it all out:** Before the conversation ends, ask, "Is there anything left unsaid?" This is one powerful question that ensures that everything has been placed on the table for discussion.

- **Change:** The worst thing you can do is listen, encourage, give hope – then do nothing to change your own behavior and performance. Compromising leaders live in a world of entitlement and denial. No-compromise leaders adapt, grow and build a culture of trust.

It is imperative that owners create an environment where **open communication on sensitive issues** can occur without fear.

Are you taking your long-term employees for granted?

The passing of time does interesting things to long-term relationships. A comfort level settles in as both you and the employee get to know and understand each other's personalities and behaviors. More importantly, all those little quirks – the positive and those annoying ones – become familiar and even anticipated. And this higher level of familiarity can, and often does, cause the leader to dial down the leadership attention that long-term employees still need, require and most of all, expect.

- **Low maintenance doesn't mean "no maintenance":** Loyal, productive and trusted long-term employees are truly a blessing for any business, but they cannot run on autopilot. Formal, thorough and scheduled performance reviews are a must. Like any employee, they need and want to know how they're doing and where they can improve. Most of all, they need your attention and affirmation that they're appreciated. A little regular maintenance goes a very long way.

- **Maintain your leadership perspective:** Your comfort level, familiarity and relationship with long-term employees can interfere with your ability to communicate what needs to be communicated. Allowing the line between leadership and friendship to become blurred can make difficult conversations even more challenging on both sides of the relationship. It is essential for no-compromise leaders to say what needs to be said – and hear what needs to be heard.

- **Avoid the double-standard trap:** This one is simple. Allowing favoritism, special privileges and different standards for select employees is an invitation for contamination to infect your culture. And you're probably compromising this most basic leadership discipline now. There can only be one standard that all employees, including you, adhere to.

- **Tap their brainpower:** Long-term employees know your business and the work from a different vantage point than you. Share responsibility with them in their areas of expertise. Give them projects to work on.

Assign them as mentors for new team members. This quote by Jack Stack says it all, "With every pair of hands, you get a free brain."

These simple no-compromise strategies can ensure a more fulfilling and productive relationship with long-term employees. They will also prevent contamination from infecting your culture because you'll never take any employee for granted. Everyone wins. 🖐

Like any employee, they need and want to know how they're doing and where they can improve. **They need your attention and affirmation** that they're appreciated.

Employees quit leaders, not companies

It seems as though the employee revolving door is spinning a bit faster these days. It sounds something like, "My company lost $160,000 in sales because these technicians quit and went down the street." And then there's all the drama, ugly words and feelings of betrayal. It's like that voice in your head keeps saying, "How could they do this to me after all I did for them?"

These situations can get so out of hand that I was once asked to be an expert witness in a lawsuit where an owner was suing his attorney for failing to properly calculate the extent of the damages. Yes, you're hurt, frustrated and angry – but this isn't about what the dearly departed did to you and your business, it's about you taking ownership for the part you played in this saga.

Employees quit leaders not companies. Personally, every job I ever quit had more to do with quitting the leader than work itself. In fact, I once quit a job I truly loved and would have stayed at for years had the leader not compromised my trust in him. Likewise, I know and accept that people quit me because of my action, inaction or behavior. It's a tough pill to swallow, but taking ownership in a employee relationship gone bad is part of being a no-compromise leader. The question is, do you learn from your mistakes?

- **Communication, dialogue and understanding:** Every employee wants and needs to know where they stand with you and the company. There is no such thing as communicating too much. If you have any employee who hasn't had a thorough performance evaluation in the past three months, you're part of the problem.

- **Never avoid performance and behavior issues:** The most serious relationship damage occurs when issues surface and conversations, because they may be tough to do, are avoided. Like any infection, performance and behavior issues only get worse – and often spread to other employees.

- **Leave nothing unsaid:** It's difficult enough to engage in a tough conversation, so why end it without getting everything out? Leaving things unsaid is simply giving permission for problems to continue.

- **Agreement on expectations and next steps:** Never end a conversation without clarity on what the expectations and next steps are – even if that means parting ways. Set timelines and check-in points to coach, reinforce and to ensure progress is being made. If you think that one conversation is going to cure everything, you're clearly part of the problem.

- **Tunnel vision is shortsighted:** Leaders are notorious for charging forward or heading off on rabbit trails. They stop paying attention to what's really going on. They become disconnected with their employees until something snaps. No-compromise leaders never disconnect from the people they lead and the customers they serve.

No-compromise leaders **never disconnect** from the people they lead and the customers they serve.

- **Culture is everything:** A toxic business culture fuels turnover. It makes it difficult to come to work. It creates resentment. The no-compromise leader is the keeper and protector of the business culture. Is there contamination in your culture?

- **Everyone seeks appreciation:** "Great job." These two little words can brighten someone's day and inspire great performance. Make the time to show and demonstrate your sincere appreciation for a job well done.

- **Sometimes, it's just over:** Employees come and go. Just like you, their needs and desires change and evolve. Sometimes they move on. Other times they quit and stay. If it's over, acknowledge it and help them move on – even if it means walking them to the door. It's all part of protecting your culture and keeping the drama outside of your company.

How to deal with difficult employees

There's no escaping it. As a leader you will have to deal with difficult employees. By "difficult," I'm referring to attitudes ranging from egotistic, entitled and self-absorbed, to disrespectful, combative and just plain arrogant. And then there are the behavior issues such as resistance to change, ignoring rules and standards, and lack of accountability.

I'm sure you know exactly what I mean because it's likely you have difficult employees on your team right now. The question is, what are you going to do about it – and when?

Difficult employees create drag and impede progress. It's like a ship trying to gain speed while dragging an anchor. The longer a leader allows the situation to continue, the more contamination spreads in the company culture. Difficult employees sap energy and divert attention away from work thereby adding unnecessary costs. Although leaders know they must engage and deal with difficult employees, too many allow these situations to continue until they go critical.

How much pain can you and your company endure? That's my response to leaders who ask me how and when to deal with difficult employees. I'm not suggesting that leaders pounce on any employee at the first sign of negative behavior. I am suggesting that leaders engage difficult employees with a measured response that begins by acknowledging that such behaviors are unacceptable. Should the behaviors continue, then leaders must ratchet up the intensity of their response. This means coaching with timelines for improvement. This process continues with clearly defined consequences until termination becomes the only solution.

- **Fear of confrontational situations:** Get over it. You're confusing "confrontation" with "coaching." As leader, it's your responsibility to help employees achieve their full potential, so the company can achieve its full potential. Engage, be respectful and coach difficult employees early.

The longer you procrastinate, the more contamination you allow into your culture.

- **Don't want to rock the boat:** The boat is already rocking. More importantly, your team sees it and are waiting for you to engage. Your leadership credibility is on the line.

- **Concern about potential lost revenue:** I hear this argument all the time. It's just an excuse not to engage. It doesn't matter how productive an employee, it's your responsibility to protect the integrity of the company and its culture – even if that requires you to terminate that high producer. Your business will recover rapidly simply because you eliminated a major source of drag and contamination.

- **Previous attempts to correct the problem haven't worked:** This one is interesting because it says the leader gave up and decided to tolerate the difficult employee. What it actually means is that the leader failed to ratchet up the coaching process to achieve resolution.

- **Procrastination:** It's an excuse. You're the leader. Engage.

- **You're just stuck:** You'll remain stuck until you sit down with your difficult employee and have that crucial conversation that's long overdue.

Difficult employees create drag and **impede progress.**

Remember, when it gets to the point where you are fighting harder to protect a difficult employee's paycheck than the employee, it's time to make a leadership decision and eliminate the drag from your culture. Allowing the situation to continue is compromise. 🐔

When your square peg can't fit your round hole

This is about performance expectations that are out of sync with capabilities and strengths. It sounds like this: "He knows what to do, so why can't he just do it?" You've said it. I've said it. Leaders are notorious for falling into the quagmire of misreading what an individual is capable of achieving.

As a result, you place otherwise competent people into positions and situations where they struggle and founder. Your frustration and dissatisfaction morphs a once confident and contributing employee into a demoralized and indifferent anchor whose weight is becoming increasingly difficult to drag along. The question is: When will you recognize that you just can't get your square peg to fit in your round hole? Will you do something about it?

One of the most fulfilling aspects of being a leader is to coach and guide individuals to reach their full potential. We love to find diamonds in the rough and shape and polish them into sparkling gems. We can never allow our belief in the capabilities of others to achieve great things to be diminished. Next to our ability to dream, innovate and envision extraordinary companies, it is our belief in the human spirit that separates no-compromise leaders from mere taskmasters.

It's when you allow your belief in the capabilities of others, shaped by your needs, priorities and objectives, without considering an individual's actual aspirations and strengths that you run into trouble. For example, you need a manager and you have a talented and high-performing employee. You proceed to "sell" this individual on the job, the possibilities and the income potential. What you're betting on is that the high performance and achievements that their natural strengths produced in one area will translate into high performance and achievements in a leadership role. Ladies and gentlemen, place your bets.

Recently I had two conversations with leaders who were so stuck in the square peg/round hole trap, they were allowing their companies to implode around them. One called me to discuss a long-term manager in whom she had invested tens of thousands of dollars in leadership and systems training. Periodic discussions to clarify expectations, concerns and next steps would show limited, short-term results.

As frustration and indifference became more apparent, the manager's attitude and demeanor deteriorated. Other employees and the leader walked on eggshells, wondering what kind of mood would appear on any given day.

After listening to story after story, I said, "I want to talk to that smart, little voice in your head. Do you truly believe that this manager will ever be able to do the job?" The answer her smart, little voice gave was, "No." We discussed how she was stuck in the square peg/round hole trap and how, in the best interest of the manager, her team and her ability to lead, she needed to put an end to the situation so all parties could move on. She agreed.

Next to our ability to dream, innovate and envision extraordinary companies, it is our **belief in the human spirit** that separates no-compromise leaders from mere taskmasters.

The other conversation was with a business owner who expanded his company and, in the process, created an opportunity for a top performer to invest in the company and buy stock. The plan was to have his new partner lead one location while he channeled his attention on the new location.

As in the previous story, he took his new partner through all kinds of business training. Well, the new location ramped up significantly slower than anticipated. Meanwhile, the partner found the accountabilities of being in charge considerably beyond her natural strengths. The partner struggled, employees got frustrated and left for greener pastures, and revenues plummeted. It was a scary and frustrating time for all.

I met with both the owner and the partner. We discussed the frustrations, challenges and leadership blockages. I coached them to build a realistic game plan. When I checked in recently, it was clear that nothing changed. The partner was the square peg and the leadership position she was in was the round hole.

Once again, I asked the owner, "If you listen to the little voice in your head, what is it telling you to do?" His little voice was suggesting that it was time to save his partner (and the business) by reassigning her to doing work where her natural abilities could thrive.

It is so easy for leaders to get stuck in these situations and to allow them to drone on for far too long. Even with the best intentions and pre-screening, leaders can still discover that an employee is in over his or her head. It's up to the leader to recognize the signs early and coach the employee to grow into the position. It's the leader who must recognize and correct the situation before the damage and costs begin to pile up. Most importantly, the leader must "save" an otherwise valuable and appreciated employee from experiencing failure in a position of responsibility he or she was not prepared for and lacked the natural abilities to succeed.

Leadership is indeed a very complex game. Do you have any square pegs that you're trying to fit into round holes?

Some things cannot be fixed.

Indifference: When 'I don't care' infects your company

Every company suffers from indifference. Without question, it is the single most toxic behavior that wreaks havoc on company cultures and performance. It can be as subtle as someone saying, "Why should I do that?" or, "That's not my job – I'm not paid to do that." Indifference also can be as blatant as people collectively refusing to follow new company procedures or systems, that sounds like, "If they're not doing it, why should I?" No matter how you view it, indifference is a poisonous behavior that can spread rapidly throughout an organization.

In business, there are two categories of indifference. The first is leadership indifference. It can be a leader who lacks compassion and respect for his or her employees. Leaders who talk down to people or reprimand in public. When a leader refuses to follow the same the rules and procedures that employees are held accountable to. It is indifference when a leader lacks concern for budgets, employee feedback systems and other essential responsibilities. Yes, indifference begins at the leadership level and the trickle down quickly becomes a raging river.

The second area of indifference resides with employees. When "I don't care" thinking surfaces in one or more employees, your company culture will begin to deteriorate. Productivity will slow and behavior issues like lateness and absenteeism will increase. If allowed to go unchecked, indifference can evolve into a major case of "destroy from within." There is no way to prevent customers from coming into contact with "I don't care" thinking.

Here's the rub: Employee indifference is a response to compromised thinking and behavior at the leadership level. If trust is compromised through breaking commitments, expect indifference. If the company vision has lost its luster, expect indifference. If employees have a reason to question your leadership values and integrity, expect indifference. If you allow double standards, unchecked egos, conflicting agendas and/or poor communication, expect indifference.

The indifference of "I don't care" often means, "You don't care enough." It means that you are not playing to your full potential as a leader. You're not communicating enough or clarifying expectations. You must address your own indifference to certain leadership responsibilities first. You must "care without restriction." You must lead by example. Your clarity and consistency – and determination to be your best – will restore trust.

Replace "I don't care" thinking with "I give my best" thinking and behavior throughout your company. Change begins with you. 🖎

When "I don't care" thinking
surfaces in one or
more employees,
your company culture
will begin to deteriorate.

When mediocrity becomes the norm

Every business has imbedded patterns of behavior that interfere with performance, quality and growth. These patterns of behavior often cause the business to wander from one challenge or crisis to another. It's when projects never get completed, goals are routinely missed and that grand vision of a world-class company slips quietly into an elusive dream. To help leaders understand why their businesses are stuck, I respectfully tell them, "You have accepted 'not good enough' as the norm in your company." For some reason, this statement seems to hit the right chord. It's like defining a company's mission as "the relentless pursuit of mediocrity."

What leaders would want mediocrity as a goal? The sad truth is that many do, not by stated intent, but through their behaviors and thinking. Addressing "not good enough" means taking action and holding everyone, including the leader, accountable to functioning as a world-class company. Complacency, procrastination and fear of rocking the boat set a high tolerance for "not good enough." And just like failure to stick to a diet or fitness routine, "not good enough" becomes the norm. It becomes an accepted behavior pattern. And it kills companies.

- **You must change first:** Leaders set the behaviors, thinking, pace and rhythm of a company culture. Don't expect others to lift up the company and rise to the challenge if you don't change first. You need to set the example. You must demonstrate your determination. No more excuses. No more procrastination.

- **Identify what you've been tolerating or avoiding:** Chances are that it's a rather short list that includes holding yourself and others accountable, lack of planning and poor communication. And don't forget those infamous crucial conversations that are long overdue. You'll never rid your company of mediocrity by avoiding the tough conversations.

- **Cheerlead your "be-the-best" change initiative:** You can't change a lethargic culture with one grand announcement at a meeting. Change initiatives require an enormous flow of information and performance data. Daily huddles, victory rallies, one-on-one reviews, coaching and mentoring – all systems must be fully turned and functioning.

- **Set a six-month Phase One plan:** Most culture shifts crash and burn in the first three to four months. By making the first six months your focus for major change, you'll be pushing your company through the hazardous "crash and burn" period. Phase Two will be the locking-in phase for new behaviors and higher levels of performance.

It's so easy to become accustomed to mediocre performance because taking action requires you and your company to get "uncomfortable." As the old saying goes, "no pain, no gain." Be the best. No compromise.

Addressing "not good enough"
means taking action and
holding everyone,
including the leader,
accountable to functioning
as a world-class company.

Leadership and creating great sculptures

Imagine taking a massive block of granite and turning it into a magnificent sculpture for all to admire. For hours you stand and stare at that granite and the possibilities of what it can become. Finally, a vision of your sculpture crystallizes in your mind. You pick up your hammer and chisel and begin to chip away. What you're actually doing is chipping away all of the granite that doesn't belong until all that remains is your work of art. The sculpture existed in the granite, but only you knew what needed to be meticulously removed to reveal it.

As a leader, you are a sculptor of great company cultures. Like the massive granite block, you take individuals with diverse backgrounds, personalities, ambitions and levels of determination and shape them into a highly functional company culture. You know that not all individuals will fit your culture. In essence, you need to chip them away. If you don't, you compromise your culture. It will never become the "work of art" you envisioned at the start. It's hard and painstaking work.

One of the most challenging aspects of coaching leaders is the "sculpting" of company cultures. Many leaders never really have a vision of what they wanted their cultures to be like. Sure, they have a company vision, but that vital view of what they want the "thinking and behaviors" of the company to be never crystallized. Simply put, without "sculpting" the right culture, the vision of the company is compromised at its core.

The more challenging aspect of coaching is working with leaders who have a wonderful vision of a company culture, but fail to do the leadership work to achieve it. This includes everything from weak hiring practices, allowing double standards and poor accountability to inadequate information flow, poorly designed systems and the failure to make tough decisions. Again, "sculpting" company cultures is tough work – but it is truly the most vital work of leadership.

My challenge for you is to become that sculptor for your company culture. Study the "raw material" you have to work with. Allow your mind to crystallize the most amazing culture that will lift your company to world-class status. Then, become the no-compromise leader and remove all that doesn't belong in your culture. You may have to let employees go because it's a safe bet some people will never fit your culture or were never properly indoctrinated into it. You will need to crank up your information flow systems. You will need to reintroduce accountability. You will need to take out that once shiny and inspiring company vision, buff it up again, and start sharing it.

In order to sculpt the company culture you want, you will need to be a true no-compromise leader. 🐓

The sculpture existed
in the granite,
but only you knew
what needed to be
meticulously removed
to reveal it.

Black holes and the dark side

It occurs in every business. It's when an individual seemingly succumbs to the dark side where negativity, resistance and defensiveness become the predominant traits. Think of it as a force field that extends about ten feet in all directions – and the last thing you want to do is to be sucked inside it. Once you're sucked in, it can take the better part of the day to purge the negativity that got all over you. The real problem is that it's not just you who's getting hit with toxic waste; it's getting all over everyone else in your company, including your customers.

Our lives can be influenced by many factors both inside and outside the workplace that can drive our attitudes over to the dark side. It affects our demeanor and body language. We can come across as always angry and frustrated. Everyone can feel it when you walk into the room as your funk begins sucking the life and energy out of it, like a black hole that consumes all matter. Star Trek fans are familiar with the Borg phrase, "Resistance is futile." Verbal communication comes across with a similar tone that "pulls down" rather than "lifts up."

Allowing negative attitudes on your team is allowing toxic waste to get all over everyone. It brings down the team, saps energy, creates drama and ultimately erodes both productivity and customer experiences. And the longer leadership waits to address the situation, the deeper the negativity spreads in the company.

- **Recognize the signs:** Negative attitudes reveal themselves through body language, facial expression and verbal communication. Just as you can see when someone is engaged and energized about work, you can identify negativity, indifference and resistance. Look for crossed arms, slumping, staring into the abyss, curt responses and disengagement. Lingering sadness and anger can be signs of personal problems, even depression.

- **Step into funk:** It's easy to simply avoid and keep your distance from negative individuals, but this strategy is not an option for leaders. In private, leaders must respectfully ask for permission to address the employee's behavior. Yes, it is difficult to have such conversations, but the consequence of avoiding them is worse. Patiently and clearly describe what you and fellow team members are experiencing. Keep the conversation safe and allow the individual to share his or her perspective as to what's causing the behavior. You may not get to the real issue, but what is important is that you acknowledged that there is a behavior problem that needs to be resolved.

- **Next steps:** Never leave an attitude conversation without agreeing to next steps. You must keep the process moving forward. Schedule another meeting in 24 hours to allow the individual to digest what you have shared. It is very likely that the individual is unaware how his or her attitude is impacting other team members. Very often, the simple process of allowing an individual to discuss or vent problems and concerns is all it takes to resolve work-related behavior issues.

- **Big problem:** If you're the one who succumbed to the dark side, you are the big problem. In coaching, my toughest challenge is working with owners and leaders who view everyone else as the problem. So, if you've been walking around aggravated, angry, depressed and verbally spewing toxic waste, it's time to acknowledge that you are the problem. In 2007, I had a bout with depression, and it was affecting my company. I got help, starting working out and found a new passion in bike riding. Looking back, the entire episode seems surreal and I will never allow myself to go there again. Leading a business is tough work. Recognize when you lose balance and get help.

- **Know when to end it:** Leaders cannot guide every individual to be a contributor and achieve his or her full potential. When efforts to address negative behavior show little or no signs of improvement, you need to make a tough decision. Allowing the toxicity to continue is not an option. There are times when it is in the best interest of the employee, the team and the company to part ways. No compromise. 🐓

Does your company have an attitude?

It seems everyone is talking about how to create dynamic business cultures – me included. While doing a Webinar on indifference and how "I don't care" thinking can slow a company down, I substituted the term "business culture" with "business attitude." Wham, the light bulbs not only turned on, they threw out some major wattage. Clearly, you understand the consequences of having employees with bad attitudes spewing toxic waste inside your company. But while you're fighting in the leadership trenches, it's easy to miss the bigger picture of what happens when customers encounter the "attitude" of your company.

Replacing the term "culture" with "attitude" simplifies the understanding of company behaviors. To understand culture, you must delve into the collective behavior of groups of people and organizations. To understand attitude, all you need to do is look at the faces and behaviors of those with whom you work.

More importantly, don't forget the face you see in the mirror. Engaging, inspiring and optimistic leaders lead engaging, inspiring and optimistic teams – and that's the attitude your customers encounter. Grumpy leaders lead grumpy teams – and that's the attitude your customers encounter. It's that simple.

- **How do you show up?** A company's attitude is a reflection of its leader. Consider how a company in the most dire of situations can change so dramatically when its leader steps up and leads the way to success. Sometimes a new leader needs to take control when the current leader is stuck and frustrated. Do you show up to win or do you show up defeated? Do you show up positive and encouraging or do you show up negative and combative? If you're blaming your employees' lackluster performance, you're blaming others for what you create.

- **Is your company caught up in its own hype?** It's so easy for a company to buy into its own "we're the best" hype. You're only the best when your customers and marketplace say you're the best. You're only the best when your competitors are all scrambling to figure out how you do what you do – and can't duplicate it. Companies that "pretend" to be the best perform like skyrockets: They shoot up high where everyone can see them – then explode.

- **What does your team think?** Schedule a roundtable meeting with employees from different areas of company to get their viewpoint on the company's attitude. Create a safe and open atmosphere for open dialogue. Keep the conversation centered on describing and defining the company's "attitude." Listen. Really listen. Schedule a meeting for the following day to develop strategies to address attitude issues that are holding the company back. Set deadlines, responsibilities and check-points before ending the meeting.

Replacing the term "culture" with "attitude" simplifies the understanding of company behaviors.

- **What do your customers think?** If you're really ready to pull back the curtain and confront your company's attitude demons, hold a customer focus group. Invite six to 12 customers to share their thoughts about your company's attitude. Again, the conversation is very different when it's focused on attitude versus culture.

It's all about creating that collective attitude for success and banishing the attitudes that attract defeat. 🐦

How to implement a culture shift

Companies are like people. They develop habits and patterns of behavior that impede productivity, slow growth, and create useless drama. And just like people, replacing bad habits and behaviors in a business with new and more efficient ones can be a daunting task. Leaders routinely discover that their best intentions to change behaviors create new challenges. So much so, leaders run smack dab into their culture's natural resistance to change. It's tough enough to change one's own habits and behaviors; changing the deeply embedded habits and behaviors of teams of people is an entirely different undertaking. They're called "culture shifts," and successfully completing one is the hallmark of the no-compromise leader.

Culture shifts are much like the Venus Flytrap. They entice you in with the promise of better times, growth and profits until you're engaged, and then it slams shut and devours you. I'm sure that any leader who has attempted a full-blown culture shift will agree with this analogy.

Don't despair. You can successfully navigate a culture shift – if you're prepared and understand the dynamics that are involved.

- **Culture shifts take time, a lot of time:** The amount of time your culture shift will take is based on three factors:

  1. **You:** Your ability to relentlessly communicate, stay focused and stay the course.

  2. **The size and complexity of your company:** This includes layers of management, departments, divisions and the geographical nature of your company, such as multiple locations or multinational operations.

  3. **The current state of your company and its culture:** Specifically, the more out of balance your business is with respect to The Four Business Outcomes, the more energy and time it will take to move it through a culture shift to no compromise.

- **You must be committed to go the distance:** It could take 12 to 24 months to completely shift a culture. Repeat: 12 to 24 months. If you're looking for a quick-fix strategy, forget it – it doesn't exist. You must be committed 100% to see this through.

- **Not everyone is going to survive the shift:** Change resisters will get on board, quit or be relieved of their obligation to work for your company. If you allow them to stay without their commitment to change, you're compromising. Compromise at the leadership level kills culture shifts.

- **Small wins add up:** Lots of small wins build momentum and unity in a culture. Celebrate even the smallest of wins. The more you celebrate, the faster the shift.

- **Sense of urgency:** You can't shift a culture without it. Find it. Fuel it. Relentlessly drive it.

They're called "culture shifts," and **successfully completing one** is the hallmark of the no-compromise leader.

Caution: I've seen companies make wonderful culture-shift strides in a matter of months. However, too many leaders misinterpret these rapid and positive "strides" as being farther along in the culture shift than they actually are. Such misinterpretations can cause you to ease up on the urgency factor far too soon, causing the culture shift to stall. Once stalled, it's extremely difficult to get a culture shift moving again. It's simply human nature for old, comfortable behaviors to snap back in a heartbeat when discipline and focus are compromised. ✎

Changing your change resisters

They slow things down. They stir the pot. They wear you down. They pull your attention away from what's important. The distractions they create cause opportunities to slip by. And, just like ducks in a shooting gallery, when you finally get rid of one, another seems to pop up. You screen applicants, have well-defined systems, and believe you're a decent leader. So how the heck do these change resisters keep finding their way into your company?

Change resisters are a product of the environment they work in. Allow that statement to sink in. As the leader, you create and are responsible for maintaining a work environment that supports your company vision, purpose and values. Your level of leadership experience doesn't matter because nurturing your company's work environment is a never-ending process.

1. **All the personalities and behaviors:** Clearly, some individuals have personalities and behaviors that are just difficult to work with. But the "difficult" part has more do with your abilities to communicate and interact with certain personalities and behaviors. You may find it challenging to interact with people who are aggressive or even passive-aggressive. Therefore, you limit your exposure to such individuals. As a result, you label them change resisters. As a leader, you need to develop the skills to interact effectively with all sorts of individuals. You need to communicate in ways both parties can listen to – and really hear.

2. **The one question most often asked by leaders:** "How many times do I have to tell them?" I bet you ask yourself that question almost daily. When expectations are poorly defined, when the "task" is missing the "why," when the follow-up and accountability is weak, you're creating the perfect environment for change resisters to surface and grow. If you think you're communicating enough, if you think your information flow systems are up to the task, think again. If change resisters are present in your company, it's time to build extreme clarity into your

communications and ratchet up the flow of information throughout your company.

3. **The consequences of tolerating change resisters:** As soon as the "can't live with them – can't live without them" justification surfaces, you are officially compromising the integrity of your company's work environment and its ability to function as a team. Any toleration immediately creates a double standard where the resisters are "enabled" to perform, behave or assume privileges that others do not. Everyone sees it. Everyone feels the unfairness. Everyone knows that you, the leader, are allowing this to continue. It's time to get the change resisters you created on the bus or drop them off at the next corner.

4. **Take ownership in the situation:** It's not "them" or someone else's fault. It's not a plot by your competitors to plant change resisters in your company to wreak havoc. It's simply a situation you created. So take a deep breath and own it, because once you own it, you've removed the biggest obstacle – you.

Change resisters are **a product of the environment** they work in.

5. **Change is constant – at least it should be:** A simple and potent strategy to prevent change resisters from popping up is to continually adapt and change your company. Change keeps things fresh. Change keeps people awake. Change can be exciting or just a necessary adjustment to remain competitive. No matter what, change avoids stagnation and boredom. Once the routine sets in, people get comfortable. And when they're comfortable for too long, change resisters get more set in their ways.

Every company has change resisters. It's what you do to help them get off the fence that matters. 🐔

Standing ovations are earned – every day

As a public speaker, I can assure you, there's nothing more fulfilling than earning a standing ovation. It's not just acknowledgment of a job well done, it's recognition for performing at a level that touches the hearts and minds of the audience in a most memorable way. When you go to a Broadway show, the performers know that the only way to earn that coveted standing ovation is to play their parts full out from curtain up to curtain down. Standing ovations are earned by giving it all you've got.

A few years ago, we were having dinner at one of my favorite restaurants. The meal was so extraordinarily wonderful that we gave our rave reviews to our waiter. Delighted to hear the accolades, he said, "The praise should really go the chef – it's his first night with us."

I replied, "Can we go into the kitchen and deliver the praise personally?" Clearly taken by surprise, he escorted us into the kitchen where the four of us said, "Bravo." There were smiles all around. I bet that chef still remembers how his opening night earned him a standing ovation.

What would it look like if a business could earn a standing ovation? Imagine your customers taking the time to stand and applaud the experience they just had interacting with your business. That would be pretty cool indeed.

Is your business going full out every day to earn such accolades? If not, why not? What's standing in the way?

- **Doing business is just like a Broadway show:** Everyone plays a role and needs to know their lines. One weak link is all it takes to reduce an extraordinary business to "average." How many of your employees show up to be contributing members of your team? How many show up as weak links – and what are you doing to address it?

- **Deliver on your promise to your customer:** Too often, there is a disconnect between the actual performance of the business and the experience it promises to deliver to its customers. Does your business deliver everything it promises, or is it blindly stuck in its own hype? Most often, it's the presence of indifference in the business culture that breaks the promise.

- **Structure, systems, accountability and commitment:** Standing ovations are the result of disciplined practice and refinement. When a business promises extraordinary experiences and quality while short-changing the employee training and development process, that's called compromise.

- **Challenge your team to go for standing ovations:** Going for the standing ovations is a non-negotiable. Don't just raise the bar – challenge your team to raise it higher. And when those standing ovations begin, you'll be able to measure it in your customer-retention rates.

Here's a final thought: Once you and your team experience regular standing ovations, assess exactly where you are. I bet you'll be at that "next level" you've been talking about. 🐦

How many of your employees show up to be **contributing members of your team?** How many show up as weak links – and what are you doing to address it?

Free your culture of compromise

To the chagrin of many leaders, the pursuit of a no-compromise culture is an ongoing, nonstop effort. Master the following 10 behaviors, and you'll be well entrenched in ensuring that compromise is eliminated from your company. Practice them daily – compromise has a nasty way of slinking back in to an unattended culture. Think of this as a cheat sheet for maintaining a no-compromise attitude.

1. **Stop tolerating the intolerable:** Period. There's funky stuff going on in your company that needs to go away – and it's your job to get rid of it. The funky stuff has to do with behaviors, thinking, entitlements, double standards, cliques, missed opportunities, procrastination, missing or failing systems, inconsistent customer experiences, indifference and so on. You complain about it all the time, but you continue to tolerate it every day. It's time to go no compromise.

2. **Leave nothing unsaid:** You're wrapping up a performance review. You discussed a whole bunch of stuff and hit on some important issues. But there's one big elephant in the living room that's been driving you crazy – and you end the review without mentioning it. You blew it. Leaving things unsaid enables inconsistent and unacceptable behaviors and performance. It's the leader's job to leave nothing unsaid because that's the only way to coach an employee to reach his or her full potential. Do it with respect, integrity and commitment to achieving the right outcomes. It's time to go no compromise.

3. **Everyone is responsible:** "They" isn't on your payroll. The instant someone on your team says or thinks, "It's not my job," that employee has made the choice to be dispensable. It takes commitment, tenacity and courage to be indispensable. Build a culture based on "everyone is responsible," and you'll redefine your definition of efficiency, productivity, sense of urgency and teamwork. It's time to go no compromise.

4. **It's only about the dream:** Your team may respect and be loyal to you, but it's the dream – your dream – that they believe in. Financial and performance reports just measure progress to making the dream a reality. Dream big. It's time to go no compromise.

5. **The relentless pursuit:** Are you deliberately leading your company on the relentless pursuit of average or mediocrity? I think not. Average is easy. In business, average wreaks of compromise. Reread resolution #1. It's time to go no compromise.

6. **Let it flow:** How many of your employees know exactly what the immediate and most critical objectives are for your business? How many clearly understand your expectations for their individual performance? How is your company's sense of urgency? The common denominator for each of these questions is "information flow." With it, there is focus, efficiency and productivity. Without it, there is frustration, fragmentation and missed opportunities. It's time to go no compromise.

Compromise has a nasty way **of slinking back in** to an unattended culture.

7. **Get off the eggshells:** Learn to identify the first "crunch." It signals that you are allowing your personal emotions, insecurities and fears to take you out of leadership mode. Leading is not about you – it's about doing what's best for the company and your employees. Keep off the eggshells. It's time to go no compromise.

8. **Your company's attitude:** Replacing the term "culture" with "attitude" simplifies the understanding of company behaviors. To understand culture, you must delve into the collective behavior of groups of people and organizations. To understand attitude, all you need to do is look at the faces and behaviors of those you work with. More importantly, don't forget the face you see in the mirror. Engaging, inspiring and

optimistic leaders lead engaging, inspiring and optimistic teams – and that's what your customers encounter. Grumpy leaders lead grumpy teams – and that's the attitude your customers encounter. It's time to go no compromise.

9. **Impatient for profit:** Profit is proof that your business model works. Profit built on integrity, purpose and high values is proof that you are worthy of being a no-compromise leader. Profit shows that you're paying attention to the company's financial reality. A history of profitability shows that growth opportunities are consistently weighed against the potential risk. Lead your company to be patient for growth and impatient for profit. It's time to go no compromise.

Average is easy.
In business,
average wreaks
of compromise.

10. **Compete on value:** Competing on price is exhausting. Competing on extraordinary value is empowering. It's a commitment to be best in class, to stand out in a crowded marketplace. What's the worst that could happen if you competed on delivering extraordinary value? No-compromise leaders are not afraid to be bold. It's time to go no compromise.

*It takes more than dressing up
as a "fearless leader"
to make you one.*

Neilism:
Leadership beliefs and thinking
must align with strategies
for measurable results to occur.

CHAPTER

Future

"Someday, I'm gonna ..."

Since my *No-Compromise Leadership* book was published, the one question I'm asked most is: How long did it take you to write it? (Not really sure I want to know exactly how long it took.) This question is most often followed by, "Someday, I'm gonna write a book." It seems that lots of people have a book inside them that they would like to write. Truth is, their books will probably never reach their fingertips on a keyboard. Their books get stuck in, "Someday, I'm gonna ..."

My book was stuck in someday for a long time. Then, one day, I removed the "someday" and locked onto, "I'm gonna write my book." I knew it was a daunting project, and today, I have a newfound respect for the term "daunting." My question for you is, what could you accomplish if you removed the "someday" from all those "Someday, I'm gonna ..." things you want to do? Could you write that book? I bet you could. Could you transform your company into that "beyond-your-wildest-dreams something you want it to be"? I bet you could – or at least get pretty darn close. It begins by ditching the "someday" and locking into the "I'm gonna ..."

I got into road biking a few years ago. I remember the first time I rode 20 miles. I fell three times that day because I was "one with my bike," and I forgot to unclip when I stopped. I made it home with my leg muscles burning, numb hands, aching shoulders and big scrapes on my left leg and arm. (I prefer to fall to my left.) The next day, I went out and did 25 miles and only fell once. A week later I did a 45-mile ride. That's when I said, "Someday, I'm gonna do a century ride (100 miles)."

The following spring, I ditched the "someday." To date, I've done four century rides. On June 19, 2010, at 5:10 a.m., I left the Harpoon Brewery in Boston with about 1,300 other insane riders to begin the 150-mile ride to the Harpoon Brewery in Windsor, Vermont – and do it in one day. The Harpoon Brewery to Brewery ride is described as "grueling" because it has more than 7,000 feet of climbing – half of which is up two mountains. They fondly call the second one The Leviathan. With nothing but "I'm gonna do this" screaming in my head, I made it over The Leviathan.

It was 2:00 p.m. I had been riding for nine hours and completed 98 miles. The temperature was in the mid 90s. The heat had sucked the life out of me. My left knee was aching. I had climbed a total of 5,298 feet and beaten The Leviathan. I had nothing left. I called it quits at the next rest stop. My bike and I hitched a ride the last 50 miles to the beer. I was 60 years old. Yes, I was disappointed that I didn't finish the ride, but I was proud of the 100 miles I was able to complete.

If "someday" preceded "I'm gonna do the Harpoon B2B ride," I never would have done it. I never would have written my book. "Someday" would have kept my book from winning the Bronze Medal in the 2010 IPPY Awards (Independent Book Publishers Award) – a level of recognition that few authors in the crowded "leadership" category ever experience.

"Someday" is just another word for procrastination and dreaming of things you'd like to do and accomplish but don't want to put the effort into. "Someday" means you don't want it enough to do the tough work, to take the risk that always precedes success, and to bet on your own capacity to stretch and do great things. Most of all, "someday" can simply mean that you don't trust yourself to go the distance.

Would all of your "somedays" fill a dumpster of maybes, hopes and dreams? "Someday" severely limits your options. It boxes you in and keeps you contained in "I-could-never-do-that" thinking. I'd rather rack up a bunch of failures to achieve something of significance. And I have racked up my share of failures.

Big deal, so I wrote a book that won an award. Big deal, so I'm crazy enough to ride my bike 100 miles. Big deal, so I built a company that's been in business for almost 20 years and helps entrepreneurs. Well, it is a big deal to me because they are my "gonna dos" and I did them. None of it was easy. There was a lot of blood, sweat and tears (especially on the bike). But I did it. I'm proud of myself, and these accomplishments give me the confidence and energy to press on – like I did cranking my way up The Leviathan. Ditch the "somedays." If you want to do something, put a pin on the map, build your plan and go for it. You'll be amazed how you will conquer your own Leviathans.

What are you building?

Stop what you're doing for a few minutes. Stop thinking about what your day is going to look like, what you need to accomplish and what challenges you need to deal with. Trust me, all that stuff will be waiting for you. Imagine your business from 30,000 feet. It's an interesting perspective because this high altitude view gets you above the fray where it's quiet and all the surrounding landscape, complete with opportunities and threats, is visible for you to study. This vantage point provides an unobstructed view of where you're taking your company. Most of all, it allows you to see if what you're building is capable of getting you there.

Too often leaders get bogged down in the daily minutia of their work. It's something akin to trying to drive the bus while keeping the kids under control and fixing the sputtering engine at the same time. It doesn't matter if you love this kind of chaotic excitement; it pulls your attention away from your ultimate no-compromise leader responsibility – to build an enduring company.

So while I have your attention up here at 30,000 feet for these few minutes, ask yourself this: "What are you building?" Describe with absolute clarity where you are taking your company. Describe what the company looks like in terms of revenue and profit. Describe what makes your company so unique that it stands alone from its competition. Describe the career and growth opportunities for all those employees who got on your bus and believe in your vision. Describe the culture you're building and how trust, integrity and respect form its foundation. Now, how do your descriptions match what you have built so far?

It frequently takes a nice big crisis to snap you out of your daily routine so you can step back and look at what you're building. It's interesting how many leaders struggle to answer with passion and clarity the question, "What are you building?" Revisit what you're building and make sure everyone on your bus gets it.

I'll conclude with this wonderful story: A gentleman saw three men laying bricks. He approached the first and asked, "What are you doing?"

Annoyed, the first man answered, "What does it look like I'm doing? I'm laying bricks!"

He walked over to the second bricklayer and asked the same question. The second man responded, "Oh, I'm making a living."

He asked the third bricklayer the same question, "What are you doing?" The third looked up, smiled and said, "I'm building a cathedral."

What are you building? 🦢

It frequently takes
a nice big crisis
**to snap you out of
your daily routine**
so you can step back
and look at
what you're building.

To build a company that endures

Imagine a business law that stated, "If you start a company, it must endure for generations." As an entrepreneur myself, I must admit that when starting a company, even Strategies, the last thing on my mind was designing it to endure for generations.

The sense of urgency is to get the doors open, start generating cash and push through the crazy, exciting and scary start-up phase. When you bet everything you have on the vision of your new company, your attention is on the here and now – not on what your company should look like long after you're gone. But what if it was mandatory that you build a company to endure for generations? How would that change your thinking?

Entrepreneurial businesses are born with a fatal flaw. They are the manifestation of their founders. As such, the separation between the founder and the company is blurred. Founder and company are one and the same. However, under the right conditions and a little bit of luck, the company can grow beyond the emotional bonds of its founder. The fatal flaw is that most start-up companies not only grow and mature with their founders – they age and die with their founders.

Is your company designed to endure for generations? Probably not. Few entrepreneurs think that far ahead. But if a law existed that required you to think far enough ahead to design your company to endure for generations, what would you do differently now?

- **Your company is not on the same lifeline as you:** You can retire one day and kick back. Your company cannot retire. Your priorities often change as you age; personal time becomes more important and precious. A company's priorities also change but in a different way. A company needs to adapt, evolve and reinvent itself to remain competitive. A company doesn't want to stop growing. It wants to get bigger, and bigger means more complexity. When your company is stuck on your lifeline, it's going to die with you. Allow your company to live its life and evolve so that you can live yours.

- **Control freaks and egos:** Apple's Steve Jobs was a control freak and had a massively brutal ego that channeled this obsession for perfection at developing innovative, amazing products. But he was also obsessed with growing an enduring company that would live on and do great things after he was gone. Good or bad, control freak and ego are part of the entrepreneurial spirit. When channeled in the right direction, these traits can propel a company to greatness. Likewise, these traits can sap the energy out of a company and create a toxic and demoralized culture. A company cannot endure for generations if the leader can't let go of some of the controls and keep his or her ego in check.

> When your company is stuck on your lifeline,
> it's going to die with you.
> **Allow your company to live its life and evolve**
> so that you can live yours.

- **You're an employee too:** You may be the ultimate decision maker, but you're also an employee of the company. Your job is to serve the company. As stockholder, your reward is profit and equity growth. By keeping an "employee" perspective, you maintain that necessary degree of separation between you and "the company." It keeps entitlement behavior under control. For example, it keeps you from using the company checkbook as your personal checkbook. This is a subtle but crucial mode of thinking that will help build a company capable of enduring for generations. It's difficult to gain respect as leader when you make it obvious that you play by different rules.

- **Excel and supplement:** If you're a "big picture" thinker and stink at managing the details, you're not alone. If you love doing the "work" of the business and find the business stuff and numbers boring or too complicated, you're not alone. If you hate confrontation and holding others accountable, you're not alone. Few leaders are the complete package. In fact, those who do seem to be a complete package, in most cases, aren't. They simply push hard in their areas of strength and supplement with the right talent in areas where they are weak. You can't build an enduring company by ignoring aspects of your company that don't interest you or that are too far outside of your natural strengths.

- **Ban mediocrity:** Accepting mediocrity in your performance or anywhere in your company is pure compromise. I view mediocrity as an affliction that leaders enable. Leaders set the standard, pace and culture of a company. If mediocrity is tolerated, it spreads like wildfire. OK is not good enough. Average is getting by. Great companies that outlive their founders have excellence as a core value.

It takes time to wrap your head around the concept of building an enduring company. The concept alone forces you to change your thinking and perspective as an entrepreneur and founder. It makes you a better leader. 🖐

*It's good to let off
a little steam.*

Growth and shifting accountability

You start a company and knight yourself fearless leader. With grit and tenacity you lead it through the exciting and sometimes terrifying start-up phase. It's like a Boeing 747 at the foot of the runway. The captain pushes the throttle to full power and the massive plane begins roaring down the runway. The commitment is made to get airborne, and in less than a minute, it defies gravity and takes hundreds of passengers on a journey to some faraway land.

At cruising altitude the captain's role shifts from taking off to leading, managing and monitoring the journey. Other accountabilities belong to the co-pilot, crew and the sophisticated air traffic control network. To have passengers, crew and equipment arrive safely at their destination, the captain must shift accountabilities to others during the journey.

A company's growth journey also requires the shifting of account-abilities to members of the leadership team. It's the only way for a leader to create sufficient separation from full-on daily engagement in company activities to focus on longer-range growth objectives and needs. One of my favorite quotes by author and businessman Jack Stack says it best: "If you're making decisions today that will affect your company in the next 30 days, you're making the wrong decisions."

Challenges and frustration typically occur when leaders fail to recognize that shifting accountabilities down to their leadership team is, in fact, a company-wide culture shift. The rush to push accountability down into the company often fails or just throws a cloud of frustration over the entire company.

1. Won't-let-go syndrome: The Peter Principle is defined as the state where one reaches his or her level of incompetence. There are leaders who, no matter how much lip service they give it, will not loosen their grip on the controls. This is one common reason why so many entrepreneurial companies grow to a point and then get stuck. It doesn't

matter how much a leader wants to grow the company, if he or she can't trust others to make good decisions and be accountable, the leader is the road block – not everyone else. Because the leader is stuck in command-and-control mode, the best the leadership team can do is maintain status quo. Until the leader looks in the mirror and really sees that he or she is the problem, nothing will change.

If you're making decisions today that will affect your company in the next 30 days, you're making the wrong decisions.

2. What-do-I-do-now syndrome: OK, so the leader understands that letting go of the controls and shifting accountability is what the company needs. The leader calls the infamous "It's time for change" leadership team meeting and lays out the new direction of the company and the distribution of accountabilities. Yes, it's a new day at XYZ Company. The meeting ends, the leadership team heads back to work – and nothing changes. It's not that people don't agree with the change – they just don't know what to do with this new level of decision-making and accountability they've been handed. Where's the road map? Where's the training and mentoring? What are the expectations beyond "get it done"? It's even more disastrous when a command-and-control leader shifts accountability because those on the receiving end interpret the move as a setup for failure. It sounds like, "Hey, if I try and do anything, our fearless leader is going interfere, change what I put my effort into, or take it over completely." Never shift accountability without a long-term plan that includes clear expectations, how much accountability you're handing over, and the necessary training and support that will set your team members up to win.

3. Who-do-I-follow-now syndrome: This syndrome is a combination of the first two. You can shift accountability but the real leadership work is in shifting employee focus to the leader who is now accountable for their work. There are all sorts of dynamics that must be overcome including employees not respecting their new leader, the new leader has poor communication skills, or something as basic as employees not wanting to lose their connection with you, so they continue to bypass the new levels of accountability.

Shifting accountability is something all leaders need to engage in if they are intent on growing their companies. The process of shifting accountability must be planned and orchestrated like any other major change initiative. Ignore it and you'll remain stuck. Rush it and you're setting yourself and your team members up for failure. The no-compromise leader prepares, communicates and executes.

Build it and they will come. Well, maybe.

Doesn't want to mess up her '8'

A business owner called upon me to help get her business "unstuck." On the surface, this was a successful business. It has a great location, impressive revenues, decent systems and a team of loyal employees. So, why is this business stuck? The answer is simple. The owner is stuck. It's a classic case of a "reluctant leader." And this affliction is more prevalent than most leaders would care to admit.

To gain a thorough understanding of where the challenges were, I met with members of the leadership team. In the true spirit of teamwork, they openly shared their concerns and recommendations for change. By mid-afternoon, the common denominator for all the challenges and frustrations was revealed.

You guessed it, the owner needed to change first. As if in perfect unison, these caring and supportive managers were saying, "We want our leader to lead us." I could see the owner's discomfort level grow as her pattern of reluctant leadership was brought out into the open.

At one point, I asked all the managers and the owner to rate the business on a scale of one to ten, with ten representing excellence. Unanimously, they all said, "We're an eight." "Interesting," I responded, "so what's keeping you from moving up the two final points to be truly world class?" We all looked to the owner and awaited her response. After a few minutes of deep contemplation, she said, "I don't want to mess up my 8." Wow! This was a profound breakthrough.

What was finally revealed here was the owner's reluctance to become a no-compromise leader. Her settling for that "8" was keeping all of her dreams just out of reach. Her settling for that "8" assured inconsistencies in the execution of work and customer service. Her settling for that "8" chipped away at accountability and dialed down the sense of urgency in the entire company. It was a commitment to being something less.

To move from that "8" to a "10" means that the boat will be rocked. It means that change will occur and everyone will be accountable. Yes, some may not like it and will fall off the boat. Chances are that they should have walked the plank a long time ago. And since this business has been stuck at an "8" for so long, it's going to require some extra rocking to get it moving again.

Yes, it was a day of breakthroughs. A loyal leadership team got to tell their leader how much they needed her to engage. An owner revealed her reluctance to lead and close the gap between something less and achieving true excellence. Together, they focused their energies on change and what it means to live the no-compromise mantra every day.

Are you afraid to mess up your "8" and be the no-compromise leader your business needs you to be? It's time for you to stand up and rock your boat before something else does it for you. 🐓

To move from that "8" to a "10" means that the boat **will be rocked.**

Increase the value
of your business

There's nothing like controlling your own destiny and being the leader of your own company. It's your show, your vision, your passion, and most importantly, it's your money on the line. Your business is an extension of who you are and how you think – and that's where lines can become blurred. Most business owners start or buy a company so they can work for themselves. But, work to what end?

The definition of an entrepreneur is someone who creates a viable business, leads and manages it to grow in value and to sell at a substantial profit. It doesn't matter if they sell it in one year or 30; the intent is to create value so that the selling price yields a major return on their investment and hard work.

So, as an entrepreneur, to what end are you working? Are you just trying to earn more money and enjoy the stature of being captain of your own ship? Or, do you have your eye on the real prize that is earned by creating value to your business?

- **Pay serious attention to your Balance Sheet:** It tells you how healthy your business is. Are you accumulating cash and assets or accumulating debt? Is your equity line positive and growing (assets are greater than liabilities) or negative and getting worse (liabilities are greater than assets)? If you can't read and understand what your Balance Sheet is telling you, learn now.

- **Stop running questionable expenses through your company:** You know exactly what I'm talking about. Stuff like vacations, clothes, college tuition payments, personal credit-card expenses or that new refrigerator. Potential buyers will interpret such practices as unethical and begin questioning all of your numbers.

- **If you're taking cash and/or paying cash wages to employees – knock it off:** It not only distorts your financial reports, it's willful intent to defraud the government.

- **Be proud of your financial reports:** If you're truly aiming at the prize, manage your company's financials so that you'd be proud to show them to a potential buyer today. If your financials tell an inaccurate or ugly story today, you've got a lot of work to do.

- **Are you your business?** Can your business function without you and the revenues you create with your own two hands? Can a buyer purchase your business today and run your company at a profit? If not, you have work to do.

- **Is your business systematized?** The better your systems, the more consistent and predictable your business is. Highly structured, systematized and accountable businesses command a higher selling price.

The definition of an entrepreneur
**is someone who creates
a viable business,**
leads and manages it
to grow in value and
to sell at a substantial profit.

There is no magic to creating a high-value business. There's only work, determination, attention to detail and accountability to the disciplines of business. What you ignore and put off today will cost you when it's time to claim your prize.

Question your 'Old Faithfuls'

Do anything in business long enough and It becomes much like Yellowstone's famous geyser, Old Faithful, that erupts every 35 to 120 minutes – it becomes normal and predictable. The problem is that nothing in business is as predictable as an Old Faithful. Your tried-and-true systems, products, services, behaviors, strategies, business model, leadership approach – even your company vision – can throw you a curve when you least expect it.

Trusting your "Old Faithfuls" to keep on keeping on is inherently dangerous. No business is immune to change or challenges from competitors that are more innovative and hungrier than you. Your trusted "secret sauce" will age and be challenged by one that's new and improved. Entirely new service and product categories will emerge making your "Old Faithful" look, well, old. It may not be in our lifetime, but someday even Yellowstone's Old Faithful will show up late, gurgle a bit and fizz out. The tourist crowds will fizz out too.

- **Think "fast or slow":** With technology, the Internet and the way social media can make or break a product – even spur the overthrow of governments – business and markets can change in a heartbeat. Given this, would you describe your company as fast or slow? If it's "fast," you're already on your game, playing hard and more capable of innovating and shifting strategies quickly. If you describe your company as "slow," complacency has already set in. Getting innovative and ramping up to outplay competition is going to be tough, if you can do it at all.

- **Think "pressure test":** "Old Faithfuls" burrow deep into a company's thinking and behavior, making them difficult to challenge, let alone change. At your next leadership team meeting, try throwing your most sacred service, product, market strategy or business practice on the table with the following statement: "I believe it's time to rethink and taking a fresh approach to _____." You'll get responses that range from utter shock to hopefully a few affirmative nods. In these economic times, it just makes sense to pressure test your tried-and-true

"Old Faithfuls" to see if it's time to upgrade or take an entirely new approach. NOTE: You need to be willing to put everything on the table to be scrutinized. Often, leaders are too personally attached to an "Old Faithful" to allow it be questioned or changed in any manner.

- **Think "shelf life":** I just threw out a bottle of salad dressing in my fridge that was well past its expiration date. The dressing looked fine, but being 10 months past the expire date was all the motivation I needed to trash it rather than try it. You need to do the same for everything and anything in your company. Things have a tendency to look and work fine when, in reality, they've grown old, stale and less effective. If it's time to chuck some of your "Old Faithfuls," do it. It's probably just the thing your company needs to shift into innovative thinking and action.

- **Accept the lessons:** Learn from your mistakes because there will be mistakes. Lessons make you better and build character. Lessons keep you humble. A lesson is just another step closer to achieving a breakthrough. Never beat yourself up for making a mistake – unless you failed to apply your lessons.

Trusting your "Old Faithfuls" to keep on keeping on **is inherently dangerous.**

- **Don't wait too long to chase your next breakthrough:** Congratulations. You achieved a breakthrough. Like any breakthrough, it eventually becomes the status quo. When you're savoring and reaping the rewards from your breakthrough, keep watching for the next trigger to initiate your quest for another breakthrough.

Surviving and thriving in the "New Normal"

The "old normal" died in the closing days of 2008. Its passing received no headlines, not even a somber obituary. It just died and took with it many of our most trusted tried-and-true business tools. We all felt its passing but few understood its significance. All we knew was that the items in our business toolbox were rendered grossly inadequate or completely ineffective. We waited for everything to calm down and return to "normal."

But things never returned to normal. The global economy and your current reality transitioned to the "New Normal." I describe "normal" as a naturally occurring standard or state where functions, occurrences and outcomes are highly predictable.

So what is this New Normal? At its core, it's driven by three absolutes: Adapt, overcome or die. The New Normal is change on steroids. And while most leaders recognize that the business game is different, they haven't adjusted how they lead, their tactics or their systems. Until you adjust and dial in your thinking, tactics and systems to meet the demands of the New Normal, your business will continue to sputter and struggle.

It's time to embrace the "New Normal." Here are some no-compromise strategies to begin your transition:

- **Lead rather than buck:** Bucking the New Normal (change) consumes more energy than leading in the New Normal. Bucking the New Normal is defensive and therefore halts progress. Leading in the New Normal is aggressive. Bucking is about excuses, blame and justification. Leading is about innovation and discovery. Put down your shields and seek understanding. That's what leaders do.

- **A rare opportunity:** There are rare times in business when unlimited growth opportunities lay before you. The New Normal is a gift not a curse. It flushes out the weak and timid. It throws open the door to new possibilities for forward thinkers and doers. The door is still open but it will gradually begin to close as this New Normal matures. Seize the moment. That's what leaders do.

- **Rally your team:** There's nothing like a shiny new vision and worthy cause to rally your team's energy. If you've been hanging on to what worked in the old normal, you and your team are likely frustrated, stressed and seriously ripe for change. Yes, change can be scary and stressful, but new visions and causes to fight for inspire hope and the belief that better, and possibly the best, times are within reach. I call it "that elusive next level." Now you have a reason to re-craft your vision and paint an extraordinary picture to inspire your team. The New Normal is about going to the next level. Take your team there. That's what leaders do.

The New Normal is change on steroids.

You can elect to fear change or embrace it. You can let go of what were once your tried-and-true business tools and challenge yourself to discover, master and even invent new ones. Step back and look at the New Normal for what it truly is – an opportunity. It's what leaders do.

Neilism:
The only thing standing in the way
of achieving your full potential is you.

You

Stop standing in your own way

Your most intelligent business advisor is usually that little voice inside your head. That voice tells you it's time to make that tough decision, to have that fierce conversation, to pay attention to your numbers and all those other things that you know need doing. It's almost comedic how that little voice inside your head knows the right thing to do. It's not so funny when you ignore it and get yourself and your company into difficult and compromising situations.

That little voice is so smart because you already know the best decisions, projects and tasks to be done. You may not know all the details, but you know and understand the basic framework. Your little voice will even coach you to be accountable, trustworthy, tenacious and consistent. What more could you ask for than to have a brilliant advisor and coach residing in your own cranium and at your beck and call 24/7?

Listening and responding to your little voice demands mental discipline – a lot of discipline. More often than not, ignoring it will lead you down the path of compromise. It's easier to procrastinate, avoid and take the easy way out than to roll up your sleeves and conquer. It's easier to be indifferent, self-centered and disrespectful than 100% committed to leading with integrity and being respectful of others. It's easier to accept "I don't care" and "average" than doing the work you know it requires to achieve your full potential – and your company's vision.

If you're tired of "average" and plugging leaks in the bottom of your ship – leaks you helped to create – stop standing in your own way and start listening to that little voice inside your head. You know you need to be accountable, to plan, to pay attention to your numbers and to live your cash-flow plan. You know that quarterly performance reviews are done quarterly, not annually. You know that avoiding today's small problems fuels tomorrow's business disasters.

If that little voice in your head knows how to get you out of your own way, that means you know what to do and what needs to get done. The only question is, will you do it? 🐓

Who can you trust?

Respect your investment

To be an entrepreneur means that you are willing to bet the ranch on your vision. You are betting on your abilities to create, lead and grow a viable business enterprise. It doesn't matter if you started your company years ago or if you're about to press the launch button, being an entrepreneur is most certainly a form of gambling. Whether your style is to play it safe and bet in measured doses or let it all ride on one big heart-thumping hand, you are responsible for your company's success or failure.

In the coaching and consulting business, we work with all sorts of leaders. We work with wild cowboys who like to live on the edge and avoid any semblance of structure, discipline and accountability to the non-negotiable rules of business. These cowboys luck out for bit, but always seem to struggle over the long haul.

At the other end of the spectrum, we work with highly structured, detail-oriented and disciplined leaders who often find their companies stifled by their inability to adapt to change and innovate. In the middle, we meet leaders who avoid responsibilities, procrastinate and get stuck in their own quagmire of compromise, resulting in contaminated cultures and one crisis after another.

Ask yourself these questions:

- **If your home,** personal assets, personal guarantee, reputation and the trust of all who believe in you are on the line, what more does it take to get you to respect your investment?

- **What will it take** for you as a leader to make the tough decisions when necessary and not avoid them until the business pain is excruciating?

- **What will it take** for you to invest time to engage with and lead your team and not hide in an office, get lost in new pet projects, or allow the work of the business to consume your time?

- **What will it take** to get you to live your cash-flow plan and pay attention to your financial reports?

- **What will it take** to get you to understand that "you" are not your company? You work for your company. You are part of the team you lead.

- **What will it take** to get you to work on the important stuff, not just the busy work?

- **What will it take** to get you to manage your time and productivity, just as you want others around you to do?

- **What will it take** for you to adhere to the same rules, standards and systems that you expect others to?

> Whether your style is
> to play it safe and
> bet in measured doses
> or let it all ride on one
> big heart-thumping hand,
> **you are responsible**
> for your company's
> success or failure.

- **What will it take** for you to look in the mirror and take ownership of the challenges your business faces?

What will it take for you to respect the money and time you have invested in your business? It's a choice that every entrepreneur makes every day. To respect is to honor. Sadly, I've seen too many entrepreneurs disrespect their companies and their role as its leader. They don't pay attention. They actively and openly practice entitlement behavior. They allow their egos to get out of control. They gamble with their family's security and the security of their employees and their families.

Yes, respecting your investment is a choice. Is it time for you to examine your choice, and change? 🦢

What part do you own?

The natural human reaction to a threat or attack is "fight or flight."
We step courageously into the fray, or we run for cover. As leaders, problems and challenges are drawn to us like pieces of metal to a magnet. Our job is to address those problems and challenges.

But somewhere between our natural tendency of "fight or flight" when threatened, attacked or confronted with problems and challenges, exists another natural human response. It's called "blame, justify and defend."

The title of my last book is *No-Compromise Leadership: A higher standard of leadership thinking and behavior.* A key element of that "higher standard" is the discipline to replace the tendency to "blame, justify and defend" with this simple question: "What part do I own in this problem or challenge?" To immediately blame, justify and defend simply triggers the fight or flight response in those you are pointing the finger at or attempting to throw under the bus. (Does anyone know why it's always a bus?)

The discipline to first explore what part of the problem or challenge you own is a sign of leadership maturity, that higher standard of leadership thinking and behavior. Did you clarify your expectations? Did you provide the necessary resources? Did you fail to deliver your part of the project on time? Great leaders, no-compromise leaders, take ownership first.

- **Maintain your leadership perspective:** A leader's responsibility is to seek clarity on all aspects of the problem or challenge. If your first response is to jump to conclusions based on superficial data and opinions, you quickly become the bus driver looking for someone to run over. Ask questions, listen intently, do your research, and be prepared to own your piece of the problem.

- **Team-driven solutions:** You'll work through problems and challenges faster by acknowledging that there was a flaw in the plan or a breakdown in accountability. It's the tried and true "we learn from our mistakes" approach to leadership. The faster you shift energy to, "Let's find a solution," you'll avoid the unnecessary drama, arguing and hurt feelings that occur when everyone plays the blame game.

- **Own only what you're responsible for:** The question, "What do you own?" doesn't mean being a martyr. Taking all responsibility for the thinking and behaviors of others will simply enable that behavior to continue. When expectations are clarified, systems are in place, accountabilities are established, and individuals still choose to play a different game, leaders must help those offenders understand what their contribution was to the problem. Enable the right behavior.

- **We are human:** Mistakes happen. The best-laid plans are always a "best guess" that the intended outcome will be achieved. I've made some pretty big and stupid mistakes in my time. I've learned and grown as a leader from most. But some mistakes took a couple of repeats before I got the thinking and behavior right. And some I'm still working on. All I can tell you is that asking myself, "What do I own in this?" has made me a better leader. It has reduced stress and drama. It has empowered my team to be self-directed. It doesn't get much better than that for a leader.

To immediately blame, justify and defend simply triggers the **fight or flight response** in those you are pointing the finger at or attempting to throw under the bus.

There's an excuse for that!

Thought of something you'd like to do on your iPhone? Voila, "there's an app for that." Yup, there are apps for just about everything and more are on the way that will do things you never dreamed possible. Like iPhone apps, when a project doesn't get done on time, when a procedure isn't followed, when a mess is left for someone else to clean up, "there's an excuse for that." There's an excuse for almost anything that gets done wrong, gets done late or doesn't get done at all.

We humans have been perfecting our excuse-making skills since childhood. While playing with other kids, remember the, "I wasn't ready," or, "My shoe was untied," excuses? By the time we get to high school, excuses have evolved to a more creative and imaginative level such as, "My dog ate my homework." When we enter the workforce, the art of excuse-making reaches the pinnacle of refinement. Here, excuses sound like, "My alarm didn't go off," or, "I didn't know," or, "I thought so-and-so was going to do it," and let's not forget the ever-popular, "It's not my job."

- **An excuse is simply justification:** Performing at a level below one's true capabilities is a choice. Excuses are attempts to justify laziness, procrastination and indifference. Excuses are a direct by-product of a bad decision or pattern of behavior.

   Strategy: Don't get sucked into the justification. It's a waste of time. Keep the conversation focused on the employee's decision and/or behavior. Ask, "What steps can you take to prevent this from happening again?" Don't end it there. Keep checking in with the employee. Correct when necessary, and give positive feedback when you see progress.

- **Excuses deflect accountability:** An employee arrives late for work and says, "I was stuck behind a school bus." Is it that darn slow-moving school bus that caused the lateness, or, an employee who didn't allow that little bit of extra time for the unexpected?

   Strategy: Creating an "accountable" company culture is the true work of the no-compromise leader. Take the employee through the ripple effect of his or her failure to be accountable to the team, the company and the customer. Clarify how even simple breakdowns in accountability can have costly repercussions throughout an organization.

- **World-class or something less:** It doesn't matter what industry you're in, just doing business in these economic times is seriously tough work. Generating growth, profitability and opportunity is even tougher. The more excuses that occur at any level of a company, the slower its progress. The more excuses pile up, the more distracted and sidetracked the company becomes as it gets further bogged down in its internal dysfunctions.

  Strategy: People fight for a worthy cause. When a company unites around a worthy cause, people engage at higher levels of performance. Why? Because they want to win. Does your company have a worthy cause to fight for? Does your company vision have the gravitational pull inspiring enough to collectively lift performance and behavior to the next level? If not, it's time to rethink and polish up your vision. Chances are, it's not motivating you either.

There's an excuse for almost anything **that gets done wrong,** gets done late or doesn't get done at all.

Here's one last strategy to consider: Are you making excuses for your own decisions and behaviors that cause you to perform below your capabilities? If so, the purging of excuses from your company begins with you. What's that you just said? "You don't have time to deal with this now." Sounds like an excuse to me. 🐓

Cynicism:
Forever your nemesis

The role of leader can be a solitary existence. You are the ultimate decision maker. You are the creator and protector of the company vision. You shape and nurture the company culture. You inspire individuals to achieve extraordinary things through the power of teamwork. You are responsible for the livelihoods and wellbeing of your employees and their families. You revel in your successes and pummel yourself with every failure. You cherish your strengths and, deep down inside, you are aware of your shortcomings. If accountability is your leadership watchword – cynicism is forever your nemesis.

Many leaders find a conflict between their own wants and needs as opposed to the wants and needs of their companies. Some leaders want to kick back and enjoy their success. Some are just so tired that they want to get out. Others want to grow their companies but resist working through their leadership blockages.

All of this emotional baggage leads to cynicism and, ultimately, feelings of resentment and entitlement. It begins to show up in your demeanor, how you communicate and your leadership behavior – and none of it is good. It's like a dark cloud that follows you everywhere. If any of this is resonating with how you're feeling, it's time to reconnect with who you are as a leader and business owner. Most of all, you must reposition where your company fits into your life. Once cynicism takes hold, it will continue to burrow deeper into your leadership thinking and behavior. Purge it now.

- **You are not your company:** When you get hardwired into every facet of your company, you're inviting cynicism. You are the leader. You are an owner, partner or stockholder. You are not your company. A company is a legal entity comprised of assets, liabilities and equity. Unlike you, a company can live on for generations. When you and your company are one and the same, it will exist according to your lifecycle. When you lose interest in it, ignore it, or abandon it – or die – it will die. Just as you transition through your leadership lifecycle, new and more energized leaders will lead your company. You are not your company. Let your company grow and evolve. That's what leaders do.

- **It's not everyone and everything else:** When cynicism grabs hold of you, it feeds on those around you in the form of blame, justification and denial. Everyone around you becomes the problem. The customers become the problem. The economy becomes the problem. You keep pushing the "do more, sell more" button and frustrate the hell out of your team. You run reports, build truly amazing spreadsheets, and bark orders, and nothing seems to work. Where's their fearless leader? Where's the vision and inspiration to achieve the extraordinary? Keep pushing the wrong buttons and you'll get frustration and stress, and see some pretty amazing employees quitting their once-fearless leader. Purge cynicism from your thinking and behavior first.

You are not your company.

- **Take a sabbatical:** Take six or seven weeks off. I bet you're thinking, "Neil has lost his mind. I can't take that much time off." Well, I took a three-month sabbatical in 2007 so I wouldn't lose my mind. I was depressed and needed to separate from my company and reconnect with my vision, goals and what achieving my full potential really meant to me. As leaders and owners, we sacrifice damn near everything for our companies. That is so wrong. That is so unhealthy. I dare you to take six or seven weeks. Bet you'll find every excuse why you can't. But what if you found every reason why you could? Find the reasons and take a sabbatical on your terms.

- **Recognize cynical thoughts:** You have them every day. They sound like, "This won't work." "We tried that before." "They don't care." "They're lazy." "I can't do that." "They'll never finish it on time." "We won't make it." "I'm the owner; I can do what I want." These thoughts lead down the road of defeat. They erode confidence and feed resentment. The secret to banishing cynical thoughts is to go positive, inspire, and innovate. You must empower yourself before you can empower others. 🐓

Is it time to take back control of your company?

Companies evolve. At any given time there are forces at work that influence the speed, performance and direction of your company – not to mention your effectiveness as a leader. The current players on your team may be just the right mix of personalities and abilities. They may be a dynamic and determined group that keeps the company energized and its culture pristine. (Every leader remembers that perfect team and how it performed.)

Likewise, your current players may not represent the best mix of personalities and abilities. Things move agonizingly slow, drama is a daily occurrence, and your job as leader just isn't fun anymore. The economy is also an ever-present force that either works for you or against you.

And then there is you, the leader. The forces of a constantly shifting company culture as employees come and go, the changing economy, and competitors that are really on their game all have an impact on how you lead. When things are humming along just right, you may get too comfortable and dial down the intensity of your game more than you should. (Just so you know, it happens to every leader.)

The question is how long will it take you to dial up your intensity and re-ignite your company's competitive fire? How long will it take to re-plot the company's course? How long will it take to make those tough decisions that didn't seem so critical in the good times?

- **Have you gotten too disconnected?** It's easy for leaders to immerse in new projects and growth endeavors. It's also easy for leaders to get lazy. When either situation occurs, the culture of the company wanders, the wrong behaviors set in and performance stalls. One of my favorite Neilisms is; "There is no auto-pilot setting for creating and maintaining sense of urgency." If you've become disconnected, it is time to take back control of your company.

- **Have you given up too much control?** With the best intentions, you may have given an individual or members of your leadership team more control and responsibility than they were prepared to assume. They may not totally understand your vision and your dream of where you want to take your company. You gave up too much control, and your company is paying dearly for it. Your company needs its leader. It's time to take back control.

- **Are you in over your head?** Were you trained to be a leader? How many entrepreneurs are fortunate to have "the right stuff" in contrast to the majority who drown in their leadership roles? It's time to learn the skills of leadership and take back control of your company.

Growing a successful business is **a high-risk** and unforgiving game.

- **Are you overwhelmed?** Growing a successful business is a high-risk and unforgiving game. You have to play all the way. You have to challenge yourself to live outside of your comfort zone. You must flip your switch from "I don't like numbers" to "I will learn and lead my company by the numbers." You must flip your switch from "I don't like confrontation" to "I coach people to reach their full potential." If you're feeling overwhelmed, your company is paying the price. Fear, self-doubt and procrastination fuel feelings of being overwhelmed. Taking steps in the right direction and experiencing positive results quickly evaporates that feeling.

Chances are that you need to take back control of your company.
Chances are that your employees are waiting for you to engage. The clock is ticking. 🐓

Watching opportunities pass you by

You watch an employee take a shortcut in a process that will create problems down the line. Your company just implemented major and much-needed customer-service standards, but some of your key employees are ignoring them. You're afraid that if you hold them accountable, they'll leave. How many opportunities to get better and grow your company do you watch pass by every day? It's most likely infinitely more than you think, and it's costing you.

My job is to work with leaders and companies to make them better – to uncover and capture opportunities. I listen to leaders talk about taking their companies to that glorious next level. I can feel their desire and intent to make serious changes, but what's often missing is the commitment and accountability to see them through.

It's no different than hearing someone say, "I'm going to start working out," or, "I'm going on a diet to shed these unwanted pounds." Fitness centers and diet programs make fortunes on people who sign up but in short order fail to show up. In business, it sounds like, "We tried that before but it didn't work." If it was a good system, process or standard of performance, why didn't it work? The real question is: Who watched it fail and why did he or she allow it to happen? It's the leader who compromised. It's the leader who watched the most recent attempt to lift the company to that next level crash and burn.

- **Stop talking "no compromise" and go no compromise:** No compromise means if it needs to be done, get it done, to hold yourself and your team accountable. Educate your team on what "no compromise" means and how it can raise the entire company to a level of success that is beyond their wildest dreams.

- **Clearly define what going no compromise will look and feel like:** Together with your team, build a "We will win" code of conduct. Revisit and reaffirm commitment to it at every daily huddle. Don't just make it a big deal for the short term; embed no-compromise thinking and behavior up to and through achieving your next level of success. Seeing a no-compromise culture emerge and solidify in a company is truly a beautiful thing.

- **Work through your fears that change will rock the boat:** Change always rocks the boat. There's a darn good chance that some of your long-time employees will balk at being held accountable to new systems, processes and standards. They got comfortable and most likely feel "entitled" to play differently than the rest of the team. You enabled it, and you need to own it. The best tactic is to be respectful of your long-time employees. They've stood by you. Help them and encourage them through the changes that no compromise requires. However, you must stay your course and prevent a double standard from occurring. If one or more just can't adapt, it may be time for them to move on. Allowing a non-player to stay is a compromise.

- **Hold yourself accountable at a level equal to the level of success you say you want:** This is the toughest part of going no compromise. If you're questioning your ability to be accountable, that means you don't trust yourself to follow through. Learn to recognize that urge to compromise and push through it. It's no different than resisting that slice of greasy pizza or not bailing on your daily trip to the gym. Living no compromise means working at it every day.

No compromise means if it needs to be done, **get it done.**

Here's the danger of compromise and watching opportunities pass you by: You get used to it. You don't like it, but you learn to accept mediocrity. We pass this way but once. If the choice is going no compromise and winning big or compromise and mediocrity, I choose no compromise. What path do you choose? 🐔

Don't allow it to get all over you

The state of the economy at home and abroad is frequently on everyone's minds. I was unsettled in 2011 by the weeks of political wrangling in Washington over the debt ceiling. The daily barrage of bickering over the nation's massive debt is never what any of us needed while we focus on leading our companies through to something that resembles an "economic recovery." And as predicted, the debt ceiling raised cataclysmic "what if's" of America defaulting on its debt.

Then, there was news of financial instability in Europe and a tanking stock market seemed to spew all over everyone like a global funk. Just as we were feeling somewhat optimistic that we had weathered the recession, feelings of financial uncertainty and fear are once again all over us.

The good news is that we have a choice to make. We can buy into the economic negativity or we can simply choose to go positive. In fact, as business leaders, we can choose to go so positive that our optimism spreads to others.

- **See the possibilities:** Every storm is followed by blue skies. It's the law of the universe. A fire will destroy a forest, but it will grow back more lush than before. Japan is recovering from the tsunami. The Great Recession was followed by years of prosperity. A new tower rose from the ashes at Ground Zero. Look for and focus on the wonderful possibilities that surround and await you. Going positive can do that.

- **Use your mind filter:** Each of us has the capacity to filter out thoughts we don't like. I'm not saying you should ignore reality; just keep it in perspective. More importantly, limit your exposure to news and data that brings you down. Going positive can do that.

- **Stay on the offensive:** Funky economic times are ripe with opportunities. While everyone else is hunkering down waiting for the other shoe to drop, get aggressive and charge forward. Keep seeking out little wins. By the time your competition realizes that there wasn't a second shoe, you'll be on fertile ground, picking away at the low-hanging fruit. Going positive can do that.

- **Lead courageously:** Flip your mental switches to positive and you'll discover a new bounce in your step. You'll find power in, "Yes, we can." Courageous leaders inspire others to rise to the challenge to achieve goals that were once considered unattainable. Going positive can do that.

> We can buy into
> the economic negativity
> or we can simply choose to
> **go positive.**

- **Believe in yourself:** So maybe things aren't perfect in your company. Maybe your credit card debt is scary. Maybe your landlord is totally uncooperative. Maybe you've had some turnover and lost some good people. Every company has stuff behind the curtain it doesn't like. But your company is alive and functioning. You survived the worst the recession could throw at you while others gave up and went out of business. Give yourself some credit. Stand tall. Be proud. Going positive can do that. 🐦

What triggers your procrastination bug?

Everyone procrastinates. Even those people you admire for their tenacity, high productivity and accomplishments are afflicted now and then with the procrastination bug. I know that I procrastinate. I have a reminder alarm that goes off every Tuesday morning at 7:30 to write my Monday Morning Wake-Up column. I often write it on Friday. I could say that I allow the ideas to bake a few days, which they sort of do, but it's much more accurate to say that I procrastinate. Do I write a better MMWU on Friday than the one I could write on Tuesday? Absolutely not. It's just me giving in to my procrastination bug.

Discovering what triggers your procrastination bug is the key to keeping it under control and practicing accountability at the highest level. No compromise is a 100% commitment to getting things done. Accountability is the foundation that no-compromise leaders stand on.

- **Know what fulfills you:** I love tasks that involve problem solving, strategy and getting into the thinking and behavior that drive business growth. I love teaching and coaching. I find it extraordinarily fulfilling speaking to and connecting with both large and small audiences. The more time I can spend on these tasks, the better I feel. What's on your list of tasks that fulfill you? Now, how does that list compare to tasks you do every day? When you engage in work and tasks you love, you naturally seek out more and achieve more. There's little room or reason for your procrastination bug to interfere.

- **Know what saps and drains you:** Repetitive and monotonous tasks drive me crazy. I also know that getting stuck in my office for days has me yearning to get back to teaching and speaking. I need diversity in my work to keep me productive. Likewise, if I'm on the road too much, I can't wait to get back into my office to write, create new content and just engage in the work of my company. If you're not engaged in what fulfills you, work becomes work, and procrastination is the easiest way to avoid it.

- **Know what's truly important:** It's hard to be accountable when your plate is overloaded. Focus on priority issues first. It's amazing how many leaders can get real busy working on low-level projects and tasks. Don't use being busy as an excuse to procrastinate on important projects.

- **Know your blockages:** Blockages are the higher-level tasks that are a necessary and essential part of your work. If you don't like numbers, financial reports and budgets, your procrastination bug is always ready to bite. If you label too many leadership conversations as hostile and avoid them, your procrastination bug has grown into one big, nasty critter. Procrastination is avoidance behavior. The problem is that avoiding leadership tasks and responsibilities almost always leads to bigger problems and challenges. FACT: You can learn and make peace with numbers. You can learn how to navigate through difficult conversations. You can break through the blockages that hold you and your company back - if you swat away that procrastination bug.

- **Know your triggers:** When you encounter situations that trigger avoidance and procrastination, shift into no-compromise mode. The longer you avoid or procrastinate on decisions, tasks or situations that cause you discomfort, the more difficult it is to engage. The best way to recognize your procrastination triggers is to listen to that wise little voice in your head. Every time your procrastination bug prepares to take a bite, that little voice never fails to say, "Hey, just get it done. Don't put it off. Do it now." The instant you hear that little voice, you have two choices: Listen and swat your procrastination bug before it bites you, or ignore it and allow your procrastinating behavior to win. And when procrastination wins out - you and all who depend on you - lose big time.

Procrastination is a conscious choice that you make. No-compromise leaders choose to "get it done." Now, how "no compromise" are you? 🐓

Overcoming leadership stress

Along with leading a company through challenging economic times comes stress. Stress from driving sales. Stress from managing expenses. Stress from keeping employees motivated and productive, and not getting caught up in the constant barrage of bad economic news. Stress from making more tough decisions and hoping they're the right ones. Yes, leadership has its privileges, but leadership can also be a pressure cooker if you don't manage your stress levels.

Stress can wear you down. Not only does it negatively impact your performance as a leader, it takes a toll on your attitude. It saps your ability to think positively. Most of all, it changes your demeanor in ways that you cannot hide from your leadership team, employees and customers. If you don't manage stress, it will manage you.

- **Focus on the positive signs of recovery:** Every down time has a recovery. It's easy to get caught up in the gloom and doom of bad times. All it takes is trickle of good economic news to begin pulling the recovery tide back in.

- **Target the next 18 months:** The heck with five-year plans; concentrate on where you want your company to be 18 months from now. What do want your company to look like on the other side of this recession? Set short-range goals and strategies to achieve them. You'll be defining your stepping stones to growth.

- **Lighten it up:** There's no better cure for stress than laughter and having some fun. Have a pizza party for lunch or company barbeque. Heck, dress like a clown. Lead an impromptu company cheer. Take your leadership team bowling or to a ball game. No contests here – you want everyone to be winner and laugh a bit.

- **Work with a coach:** It's well documented that the best leaders use a coach. A good business coach will keep you sharp, focused and hold you accountable for making progress. You'll have a sounding board for your ideas and that ever-important outlet when you need to vent.

- **Take time to appreciate your achievements:** If you're in business today, you're doing something right. Step back and acknowledge the things you did well and the things you did right. Don't give energy to the bad decisions. Doing so fuels stress.

Step back and acknowledge
the things you did well
and the things you did right.

Leadership and happiness

Along with being the leader of a company comes a whirlwind of feelings, and somewhere intertwined in those feelings is happiness. I'm referring to the joy one experiences serving as the leader of a company or organization. And the reason I'm focusing on happiness is simple. In the daily process of leadership, happiness can easily get relegated to a "wish I had it" rather than "I gotta have it" feeling.

Why be a leader if it doesn't make you happy? Why put yourself into situations that cause stress and even extreme distress? Why subject yourself to criticism from those who don't agree with how you lead?

So where exactly is the happiness part of leadership? The answer is basic: It's all around you. You're just too caught up in the decisions, frustrations, challenges, misfires and backfires to see it. You may be questioning your own leadership abilities, or style of leadership, or battling your own leadership blockages, such as fear of confrontation, or the all-time favorite – procrastination. Yes, it's hard to find happiness in leadership with all this stuff going on around you and inside you.

You're probably thinking of asking the business gods, "Please send me some leadership happiness – now." Remember what I wrote earlier – happiness is all around you; you just can't see it.

- **It's really about people:** Numbers just measure your effectiveness as a leader. If your company culture has toxic waste building up, or if it's in the fiery pits of hell, your numbers will reflect it. Leaders are the keepers and protectors of the company vision. Leaders inspire others to reach their full potential. If you want to find happiness, make paying attention to your people your top priority. Lift your team up and show them the path to that elusive next level that you want to get to. Flip your mental switches to "positive" and sparks of happiness will begin to appear.

- **Celebrate the good:** It's so easy to become consumed with all that's wrong with your company that it clouds all that's good about it. Here's one to start with: If you're still in business today, your company is surviving in the worst economic times since the Great Depression. Even if your company is struggling, it is alive and functioning. It had a "win" somewhere. Did you celebrate it? An employee rose to the challenge. Did you celebrate it? You made a tough decision. Did you celebrate it? It's hard for people to step up and make a difference when the leader forgets how to give a high-five or shout out a "woo hoo." There is happiness occurring all around you. Take the blinders off and celebrate every morsel of it.

- **Get it done:** There is something about checking off "big items" on your to-do list. By "big items" I'm referring to those infamous tough decisions that you know must be made but that you avoid, ignore and procrastinate on. It's hard to find happiness when you're stressed and agonizing over a tough decision. It's even worse when you've made the decision but refuse to hit the launch button. In almost every case, happiness resides on the other side of tough decisions. Fulfillment is derived from getting things done. Happiness is the glow of fulfillment. Get it done. Be happy.

The mood of the leader **sets the tone** of the entire company.

- **Lighten up:** The mood of the leader sets the tone of the entire company. I've seen leaders enter a room and instantly fill it with their funk. When you're in a funk, you bring it with you wherever you go and get it all over everyone else. You can even spread your funk on the phone, in e-mails and in text messages. There are certainly times when leaders need to be serious. But as keeper of the company culture, you need to lighten up to lift your company up. No compromise.

To be everything – including what you're not

If you had to describe your role as a leader, what would you say? What's interesting about this question is that every leader will offer a slightly different perspective that is unique to his or her abilities and experiences. Some revel in the thrill of leading a start-up or turnaround only to find boredom and frustration in the day-to-day running of the business. Some leaders are innovative visionaries who can see opportunities where others do not. There are leaders who can communicate with extreme clarity and purpose while others struggle to find the right words. There are leaders who master the process of having challenging conversations while others dread and avoid them. And there are leaders who love data, numbers, systems and structure while others find them confusing and confining. The list goes on.

I bet you have high expectations for yourself as a leader – and you should. You must envision, guide, mentor, plan, solve, track, analyze, praise, discipline, inspire, understand, be accountable, hold others accountable, make tough decisions, drive sales, create profit, manage cash flow, be compassionate, and create just the right company culture. I don't know about you, but I felt my stress level increase just writing this. It's as if the title "leader" is to somehow magically bestow all the qualities of a great leader upon you. But alas, leaders are not superheroes. They're simply individuals with the drive to find their own version of fulfillment at the top of the success ladder. The crowded middle and lower rungs just don't do it.

If you're one of those leaders striving to be a "complete package," consider what you are demanding of yourself. True, some leaders have a lot of the right stuff – but they don't have it all. Even the most admired and successful leaders can hand you a wish list of traits and abilities that would make them more effective.

Great leaders recognize that they are not complete packages. They focus on their strengths because that's where they can make a difference. However, they don't ignore their leadership weaknesses. In fact, they work hard at getting proficient in skills and abilities that are essential to their leadership role. What they don't do is channel energy to those abilities that they know are best left to others who possess them as strengths. Great leaders who appear to be complete packages are the ones who fill in the gaps with the strengths of others.

Leaders who attempt to be complete packages, especially when they know they are not, lead mediocre companies that achieve mediocre success. They are essentially pretending to be complete. They procrastinate or ignore those elements of business they find uninteresting or confusing. Whether it's ego or distrust to share responsibility, the end result is that the business suffers.

To be everything as a leader, including what you're not, you must surround yourself with the right talent to fill in your leadership ability gaps. Doing so will free you to engage in the work that feeds your passion and leads to fulfillment.

Even the most admired and successful leaders can hand you **a wish list of traits and abilities** that would make them more effective.

Take a moment to assess how complete you are as a leader. Identify where your abilities need the support of others. Share responsibility and you will discover that you can be everything as a leader – including what you're not.

Knowing when it's time to find your replacement

Many articles have been written about the lifecycle of a business. It begins with the exhilaration of the start-up phase and pushing your way through survival mode, achieving self-sustainability, and ultimately, becoming a mature and enduring company. Yes, many businesses never make it through survival mode, but for those that do, their founders also journey through their own leadership lifecycle. And one of the most perplexing challenges of that leadership lifecycle is when founders recognize that, in order for their company to endure, it's time to find their replacement. Here begins a period of working through complex emotions and perhaps the most important decision a founder will ever make. The only way to bypass this period is to sell your company or discover the fountain of youth and become immortal.

I know that many of my natural abilities, like public speaking, writing, coaching and knowledge of how business works, has pushed and pulled Strategies through its own lifecycle. I am well into the process of preparing myself to find my replacement and turn over the reins of my company. As a lifelong entrepreneur, it is very much about preparing yourself mentally and emotionally for this inevitable transition of authority and accountability.

- **Your replacement will be a different leader than you:** If you think you're going to find a replacement that is a clone of you, forget it. It's likely that what your company needs is not "another you" to lead and grow it. A mature company requires a leader who is more strategic and disciplined than entrepreneurial. The reason is simple – a mature company is more complex. It has more "moving parts" that require structure. Entrepreneurs are visionaries who love to create and build things. Look for a replacement with the skill set to take your company further than you were able to. Don't look for a clone.

- **Don't rush the process and never settle:** You are going to be transitioning the authority to run your company to another person. It is best to proceed slowly and diligently. Clarify your expectations for the position and what your role is going to be. Share information on your company thoroughly and openly – that means pulling back the curtain for your potential successor to see and understand the good, the bad and the ugly. Better to have a candidate withdraw from consideration rather than quit a few months in. Each step will determine if you should move to the next step or stop the process. It's all about the exploration to ensure a good fit because you want more than an administrator – you want someone who is passionate about the work of your company and wants to grow it.

It's about preparing yourself
mentally and emotionally
for this inevitable transition
of authority and accountability.

- **Reconnect with your strengths and your passions:** There are aspects of your work that light you up and feed your passion. Take time to rediscover and connect with work that makes you feel wonderfully fulfilled. The opportunity to engage in work you love without the day-to-day responsibility of running your company is waiting for you. You earned it – so go for it.

- **Begin wrapping your head around your new role:** A company cannot have two presidents. You'll just frustrate your new leader as well as the rest of your team. You can't transition your leadership authority to your replacement without letting go of the reins. This means you will be shifting into a period of mentoring your new leader and gradually letting go as confidence builds. The transition takes time, so give it time.

How big is your decision?

A Webinar speaker did a long-winded buildup to what he guaranteed was "the one question no one ever asked you." Finally, he asked the question: "What is the name of the person who gave you permission to think and go big?" He said it was his wife. And after getting permission, he skyrocketed as an author and speaker in the areas of sales and Internet marketing.

Thirty minutes into this webinar, I found myself desperately seeking something of value when it hit me. The speaker's big question was wrong. No one has to give you permission to think and go big. It's your decision – and yours alone.

- **You created your current reality:** Saying "I can't" or "I'm not good enough" are thoughts that manifest behaviors that hold you back. If people around you say "you can't" or "you're not good enough," it's your choice to either buy into that thinking or prove them wrong. You can change your thoughts any time you choose. Want to change your current reality? Think differently. Think big.

- **Your potential for thinking and going big is limitless:** I've always wanted to go to China. I got close six years ago. I went to Taipei, Taiwan, to do a seminar where I became friends with my interpreter, Wanda. She gave me a lead for a keynote opportunity in Beijing that I instantly went after. The conference organizer produces events globally for a wide array of industries. I spoke in Beijing in 2011, fulfilling a dream.

- **Thinking big is just the first step:** Give yourself permission to think big and a whole new world of opportunity opens up before you. Taking action requires courage and determination. Fear of failure, fear of the unknown and doubt are nothing more than self-imposed excuses for not taking action. You're holding yourself back. I have failed many times – because I took action. I truly believe that my failures have made me successful. There isn't a success story ever told that wasn't built on a string of failures.

- **Create your own gravity:** When you think big and take action to go big, things start to happen. You gain ground. People begin taking notice of you and your work. You become an authority – the go-to person or company. The value of what you created increases exponentially. In essence, you created your own gravity that attracts the best people and opportunities. Warning: Gravity can also attract things you don't want – and that usually occurs when you stop paying attention.

So I guess we all got something of value out of that Webinar, after all. Now, think big and take action to go big. No compromise. ✒

No one has to give you permission **to think and go big.** It's your decision – and yours alone.

What's your exit strategy?

Lately, it seems that the two questions I'm being asked most are: How do I figure out what my business is worth, and can you help me create an exit strategy? Clearly the frequency to which I'm receiving such questions has a lot to do with baby-boomer business owners confronting the reality of what to do at this stage of their careers. Yes, that day will come when you too must decide on an exit strategy from your business.

All entrepreneurs eventually must separate from their businesses and move on to a new phase of life. This doesn't mean you have to stop working and retire. You may have other interests to pursue that will tap your years of experience. Heck, there's nothing wrong with just kicking back enjoying life after years of hard work.

But here's the rub. "Cashing out" and walking away from your business with a big smile on your face isn't going to just happen. I've been in this industry many years and I've only seen a handful of fortunate and prepared owners cash out and have that big smile. They had an exit strategy or ran their businesses aggressively and diligently to build value.

- **It's never too early or too late to plan:** Where do you want your business to be in five or ten years? What do you want it to look like? How much in revenues and profit? Planning means setting a future goal and creating the necessary steps to achieve it. If you don't like to plan – don't expect a windfall when it's time to sell.

- **Financial reports tell a story:** Today, right now, what kind of story do your financial reports tell? "Action adventure" where the hero gets the girl and the gold? "Drama" where it's life and death all the way. "Horror" where there's lots of scary stuff, guys with hockey masks and chainsaws? Make sure your financial reports tell the story you want today and they'll reward you tomorrow.

- **Is it a business or you?** This one is simple. If your business can function profitably without you generating revenue with your own two hands, you're on the right path. If not, it's time to rethink the design of your business and your role in it.

- **Is there a natural successor?** If you have a son or daughter in the business, are you grooming them to take over or will it require the jaws-of-life to pull control away from you? Is there a key employee worthy, capable and with the resources to acquire the business?

Your business most likely represents your life's work. Given this, it deserves to know what will happen to it when you decide to move on to the next phase of your life. Drafting a simple initial exit plan based on the previous points is a good starting point. From there, it can be refined into something more detailed and concrete. Consider working with a coach to construct your exit plan. Constructing an exit plan today can give you many fine days of barbeques and beer-sipping after you sell your business. ♞

If you don't like to plan – **don't expect a windfall** when it's time to sell.

Making the most of your 'time slot'

Time is the most precious thing in our lives. Although time itself will continue to tick away indefinitely, for us mere mortals, our time is finite. We have a beginning and an end – like our own personal "time slot." Some choose to do great things with their time slot, while others talk about what they're going to do but don't gain much ground.

We never seem to have enough time to accomplish all the things we want to do. That's what it usually feels like these days. We're living in extraordinary times. Things move fast. Every day, all day, information comes at us in massive quantities. Business moves at a relentless pace. And in these economic times, being on your game every day isn't just the way it is; it's the way it has to be.

- **It's your time slot to do with as you wish:** I need to live my own dreams and follow my own path. If someone chooses to procrastinate his or her way through life, that's the choice that's made. If you want to go after your dreams and are willing to give it all you've got, that's also a choice. I cannot fathom the thought of wasting away my time slot with dreams that I never go after.

- **Live up to your own expectations:** You can spend your life trying to live up to everyone else's expectations, or, you can live up to your own. I may be motivated by others to stretch, but I'm my own best motivator. I know when I'm on my game and when I'm not. I know when I'm working on high-value projects and when I'm just keeping busy – knowing that "keeping busy" is another form of procrastination. Live up to your own expectations and you'll exceed everyone else's.

- **It's OK to take "me time":** None of us is endowed with super-hero powers. I need to balance periods of intense work with "me time." That's why getting out on my road bike every few days is so important. It gives me time to think or just zone out. I feel great after. And it keeps me fit, both physically and mentally. If you're feeling burnt out, it's usually because you're not balancing work with taking care of yourself.

- **Work your bucket list:** I know that there are some big items on my bucket list that just may not happen. I also know that I'm the reason those things won't happen. I know that if I want them enough, I'll go after them. Writing *No-Compromise Leadership* was on my bucket list for years – until I finally decided it was time. No matter what, I keep adding to my bucket list and checking items off.

I hope this gets you thinking about what to do with your own time slot. It got me thinking about mine. 🐦

You can spend your life
trying to live up to
everyone else's expectations,
or, you can live up
to your own.

The secret to getting less of what you don't want

Make a quick mental list of all that stuff you would like less of in business and as a leader. I bet you'd like less aggravation and stress, fewer employee problems, lower payroll costs, less waste, less debt, less on your plate and so on. It can be pretty freaky how quickly your "I want less of" list can morph into one big knot in your stomach. But fear not, like Speedy Alka Seltzer, I bring you the secret to instant relief.

Before I share the secret to getting less of what you don't want, I need to warn you of some potential known side effects of use. You may experience feelings of anxiety that can dissipate rapidly by taking action. You may feel the desire to cast blame on others until you figure out who really needs to take ownership. You may experience intense euphoria when you realize that you create all of the stuff you don't like and have the power to make most of it go away.

OK, here are the steps to getting less of what you don't want:

- **Step One:** Step One is simply a reality check. You cannot be in a leadership role and be surrounded only by the good things and the stuff you like. I've devoted my life to studying, writing and teaching leadership, and I still have stuff around me that I'd like to have less of. I truly believe that a life without stuff that drives you crazy would be boring. Life and leadership are about working through challenges. There is no "easy button" in leadership. If you want an easy job, get out of leadership.

- **Step Two:** Marvel at your ability to create, directly or indirectly, all of the things you want less of. Yes, it's pretty darn amazing to realize that you had a hand in creating all the stuff you want less of. Aggravation and stress are by-products of poor and/or risky decisions, avoiding what your financials and critical numbers are telling you, poorly defined expectations, lack of leadership and its evil twin – micromanagement. The secret to Step Two is knowing that you have the power to create stuff you want less of, and therefore, you have the power to make that stuff go away.

- **Step Three:** Begin your journey to having more of what you do want in your life. There is something invigorating and empowering about starting a journey to a better place. Step Three is about making your choice to begin your journey away from the stuff you want less of and filling those voids with the stuff you want. Tired of missing goal? Channel your creative powers to innovating ways to win, ways to inspire yourself and your team. Tired of employee problems? Peel back the layers, find the problems and innovate ways to fix them and achieve the right outcomes. Step Three is about taking action.

- **Step Four:** Stay the course. I mean really stay the course. Too many leaders opt for the quick fix, making declarations such as, "Things are going to change around here." The recurring pattern is the big launch followed by a short hang time. If your employees have ever said, "We tried that before," the message they're sending is that you don't stay the course.

There is no "easy button"
in leadership.
If you want an easy job,
get out of leadership.

So, the secret to getting less of what you don't want and more of what you do is all about you, the choices you make and the actions you take. Now, start getting rid of that stuff you don't want and replace it with more of what fulfills you. No compromise. 🐓

Stop. Breathe. Appreciate.

Leading a company is tough work. You're where the buck stops. You make the big (often difficult) decisions. You mentally take your business home with you at night and wake up with it in the morning. You're a perpetual problem solver, motivator, disciplinarian, mentor, policy maker, cash-flow manager, innovator, friend, strategist and more. Yup, you're a leader, and you probably wouldn't have it any other way.

One of the seldom-discussed issues of leadership is how the "business of leadership" can consume your thoughts, emotions and energy. You know what I'm referring to. It's that feeling of being hard-wired into your business. It's that need to keep pressing forward, to find those keys that unlock doors to new opportunities. I'm not trying to stress you out here. I'm just describing what all leaders internalize.

As leaders, we need to learn how to manage and cope with the pressure and stress, or otherwise drift into burnout. We need to recharge our batteries by intentionally stepping out of the leadership pressure cooker. I'm not talking about taking vacations or long weekends; I'm talking about a few minutes of deep thought that lifts you above the turbulence that surrounds you every day.

1. **Stop:** I mean stop everything. Close your office door and put your phone on "do not disturb." How about getting out of your business and going to a park or other place where you can take in nature? I live near the Connecticut River and Long Island Sound where there are some spectacular places to just sit and take in the water views. It's even better when I'm out riding my bike through such scenic places. The point is to stop being "the leader" for a few minutes and be "you," to decompress. Remember, you are not your business. Your business is simply something you created. This separation is necessary to achieve balance.

2. **Breathe:** Take in a few deep breaths. This forces you to concentrate on your breathing rather than the thoughts swirling around that brain of yours. If you followed step one and really "stopped," deep breathing will relax you and prepare you for step three.

3. **Appreciate:** I mean really appreciate. "Appreciate what?" you ask. How about appreciating your business, your employees, your customers and all those who support and make your company what it is? No business is perfection, so appreciate its rough edges and imperfections. Guess what? By taking time to appreciate all of the good that exists in your business, chances are that you'll find a few of those keys to unlocking the new opportunities you've been seeking. How about just appreciating life? Life is a pretty amazing thing.

We need to
recharge our batteries
by intentionally
stepping out of
the leadership
pressure cooker.

I'm an entrepreneur. I get frustrated at my business too. And every time I stop, breathe and appreciate, I feel better and see things more clearly. I discover solutions and opportunities that I just couldn't see when up to my eyeballs in my own leadership pressure cooker. Give these three simple strategies a shot and you'll see what I mean. I did this morning. That's why I wrote this. 🐦

Why leaders obsess – and what to do about it

It's our job as leaders to obsess. In fact, if we weren't obsessing about something, we'd obsess the fact that we have nothing to obsess over. If you think about it, obsessing is much like your shadow: It follows you everywhere. We obsess about all kinds of stuff, some of which is actually worthy, even critical, to obsess over. And then there's all that low-level interference stuff you obsess over even though you'd be hard-pressed to explain why.

I am proud to admit that right now I'm obsessing over a few big projects I have on my plate: sales, cash flow, challenges coaching clients are having, ramping up new coaches, and so on. Yup, I always like to have my "things I'm obsessing over plate" nice and full. You're probably thinking, "Hey, my obsessing plate is just like Neil's."

I'm also obsessed about writing the Monday Morning Wake-Up that I need to write immediately after this one, whether the capacity of the 3-hole punch tray in the new printer we're testing will meet our needs, that for the first time this year I do not have a flight booked to anywhere, whether we'll have good weather next June for the MS Cape Cod Getaway Ride, will I like the new salt and pepper grinder set I just ordered, if Republicans and Democrats could agree on what today's date is, and other truly worthless mind garbage. One more thing - I obsess over e-mail. I hate when it piles up. Drives me crazy. So I check it all the time. Now that I think about it, I think I check e-mail just to take a break from obsessing about other stuff.

- **Essential obsessing:** Leaders obsess because our decisions impact the lives of others. It's our job to make the tough decisions to grow our companies. Those decisions may take away a family's primary source of income or jeopardize our personal assets. Tough situations and decisions keep you awake at night. It's the stress that comes with the job.

Essential obsessing is best described as the process of critical thinking where issues are defined, options assessed, and the best decisions made.

- **Non-essential obsessing:** Hey, it's OK to obsess about the little things - but not if you're doing it to avoid obsessing about the essential stuff. And here's a thought that will make your day: Think about what would happen if you didn't waste time obsessing about the little stuff. The only thing that would happen is your attitude and outlook would probably find their way to a state that is less stressful, lighter and – if you can handle it - more enjoyable. If anything, it will give you more time to do some high-quality obsessing about the essential stuff.

- **Decisions and actions:** Obsessing usually ends when the decision is made and action is taken. Even if the decision is the best from a list of tough options, the decision itself triggers your stress-relief valve. Taking action is like working out. It gets your body moving and your heart pumping, making you more productive and moving you toward your objective.

- **It's a choice:** I'm an "obsessor." I know it - and so do the people in my inner circle. And I know I can control it. I can turn it off, if I want to. But doesn't that sound like an excuse to keep on obsessing to my heart attack's content? It sure does. The true answer is that I can control my obsessing nature if I give myself permission not to obsess. Give yourself permission to do stress-relieving things; it's an amazing gift. I feel less stress just writing this.

- **Driving them crazy:** Hey, if we know our obsessing is driving our employees crazy, let's do them a favor and get it under control. You're not going to get better results stressing everyone out. Leadership is about inspiring others to achieve their full potential so you can achieve yours. 🐓

ANALYSIS
SOLUTION
PROCESS
OBJECTIVES
TEAMWORK
VISION
SALES

Neilism:
Strategies are the breadcrumbs
that lead you to your vision.

Strategies

Ensuring 'quality of life' for your business

As individuals, we make choices regarding how we choose to live our lives. As spouses and parents, we make choices regarding family, lifestyle and how to raise our children. But leading a company is an entirely different responsibility. Every action you take, every decision you make, how you show up at work every day, how you praise, how you discipline and how you step up and lead your company through the inevitable challenges it will encounter, dictate the quality of life of your business.

When a business meanders from one crisis to the next, its quality of life is compromised. Whether it's a cash crisis, performance crisis, or contaminated culture crisis, there is a leader who "led" it there. In contrast, when a business is thriving, dynamic and profitable, there is a leader who led it there through good decisions, a sense of urgency and accountability to the vision.

How would you describe the quality of life you created for your business? Is it inspiring, engaging, nurturing, courageous, determined and prosperous for you and your employees? If it's anything less, consider the following:

- **Are you leading and really in the game?** Challenging economic times and the general stress of leading a business can wear you down and cause you to withdraw. It's time to snap out of it and rekindle your passion for leadership. How do you snap out of it? The first step is to take ownership of the situations you created. Otherwise, you'll just be firing blame off on everyone and everything around you.

- **Define what you are building:** Why did you start your company? Why did you want to be a leader? What were the rewards you were seeking? You must be able to define what you want your business to provide in order to achieve it.

- **Define the quality of life you want for your business:** This is high-level thinking that you need to immerse yourself in. I'm not talking just profitability and making money. Making money is an outcome. Dig deep to define the principles, values, opportunities, engagement and how your company can provide extraordinary futures for you and every employee. Lead your company to a better place. Stop wallowing in your current reality.

- **Get in touch with your passion to do great things:** Leaders do great things. Leaders keep the clarity of the vision alive. Leaders keep the drumbeat steady to maintain momentum. Leaders lift their teams when they're down. Leaders take their companies to a better place. Raising the bar to achieve that infamous "next level" grabs everyone's attention. It delivers a challenge worthy of the entire company's efforts. What's "great" for you? 🦃

Leaders take their companies to **a better place.**

Recharge your business every 90 days – or more often

As a true Aquarian, I often find myself dreaming about doing great things. By great things, I'm talking about endeavors that make a difference in the lives of others. My lifelong passion is teaching, coaching and writing about leadership, and helping grow dynamic companies. One key observation is that every significant gain in business performance can be narrowed down to a concentrated period of vision refinement followed by leadership decision-making and intense implementation. I'm talking about change initiatives big enough to grab the attention of every team member, an all-hands-on-deck, company-wide call to action.

It took General Motors about 90 days to snap out of its "We're the biggest" stupor and reconfigure itself to compete in a very different economy. Unfortunately, GM needed a major recession as its wake-up call. A crisis is always the perfect catalyst for change, but just ponder the growth and performance opportunities if you built one or more significant recharge initiatives into your yearly plan. The magic of an entrepreneurial business is its agility to adapt and change quickly, if its leader is willing to initiate and lead the charge. Are you?

- **Business routines get stale and slow:** New projects and change initiatives fuel a company's sense of urgency. But new project and change initiatives eventually become just part of the daily routine – if they don't die along the way. When was the last time you grabbed everyone's attention by intentionally rocking your company's boat? If it's been six months or more, the excitement is pretty much gone. If it survived implementation, it is now just part of the routine. True, you may have gained measurable results, but how long will the momentum last? It's time to recharge.

- **Recharge what?** Maybe what needs to be recharged first is you. It's easy for leaders to coast a bit or even "check out." Are you showing up every day as the leader of your company or something less? Are you at the helm steering your ship or letting it run on autopilot? If someone else is steering your ship, is it going in the direction you want it to go, as fast as you want it go? I've seen too many leaders disengage or get so wrapped up in "their" work or projects, only to find their companies drifting aimlessly. I bet there's a big project waiting for you on that procrastination back burner of yours. Go for it.

- **It doesn't matter how successful your company is right now, there are one or two things that have been poking at you to address.** Maybe it's a productivity challenge, budgeting or cost-cutting initiative, revamping your company's information-flow systems, or an overhaul of your customer-service systems. Fact is, you've got a fine laundry list of projects to tackle that can recharge your company. It's OK to rock the boat a little every 90 days or so. It wakes people up and energizes your company's performance. Most of all, when planned recharges become the norm, resistance to change becomes a non-issue. That alone is reason enough to recharge.

- **Push it across the finish line in 90 days.** When you channel team efforts to complete a major change initiative within 90 days, it creates a natural sense of urgency that breaks through barriers that slow, stall or kill a recharge effort. Come on, push it. Rock the boat.

Are you showing up every day **as the leader of your company** or something less?

These are crazy times to be in business. The landscape is changing daily. Everyone is tweeting his or her message. Facebook is the new global meeting where your employees, customers and competitors are making friends and having conversations. Competitors are just waiting for you to let your guard down so they can scavenge your market share. If your company isn't recharging every 90 days or sooner, it's losing momentum. 🐦

Beware of 'sound bite' solutions

Having performance issues with an employee? Just Google a solution. Stuck on that tough business decision? Just post a question on a zillion different discussion groups. Looking for some insights on a particular topic? Just attend a 60-minute Webinar – or a breakout class at a trade show – rather than attend a multi-day seminar where you'll get all the information and hands-on learning you really need.

My sound-bite warning applies to book summaries too. As an author myself, I can tell you that it's impossible to get the full meaning, message and essence of a book through a Cliff Notes summary. It's like comparing a Twitter tweet to a comprehensive white paper. One is a thought. The other is detailed research. Would you consider making a business decision based on a 140-character tweet? I hope not – even if that tweet leads you to another "sound bite" of information.

Having unlimited access to an ever-expanding resource of global knowledge is a mixed blessing. Within seconds you can be reading a possible solution to a problem or that missing link to complete your latest innovation. But are you reading sound bites? Is that response to a discussion group post a solution that worked for someone else's business – but may not work for yours?

In this age of instant information, the danger of sound-bite solutions is to confuse them with real solutions based on data, research and documented outcomes.

- **View sound bites as breadcrumbs:** That's all they are – breadcrumbs that may lead you to a solution that will work for you.

- **Research takes work:** If you're looking for shortcuts and quick fixes, try feeding your company some of those breadcrumbs you found and see what happens. If your company needs a complete change of diet and three square meals a day, those breadcrumbs won't go very far.

- **Quick fixes are nothing more than duct tape:** I've been in the coaching and consulting business most of my working career. Not a day goes by without a leader asking for a quick fix. Here's my favorite: "I have an employee who's doing big numbers. How much should I pay her?" My response is usually, "I'd pay her $100,000." Then I get, "But I can't afford that!" Then I ask, "What can you afford?" From there we can drill down to the financial and budgetary issues that represent one aspect of awarding a pay raise.

The danger of sound-bite solutions is to confuse them with **real solutions.**

- **The right solution may require an investment:** It all depends on the nature and gravity of the problem. If you're not good with numbers, you may need a coach with the financial know-how to get you to a solution. Maybe it's hiring a coach, working with a mentor – or investing the time and money to get into a seminar or business program where you can get what you need. We hear, "It's not in the cash flow," all the time. But the problem is costing you money today, tomorrow and the day after. How long will it take you to find the solution on your own? Investing in the right resource will likely cost you far less than the financial bleeding that's going on.

This is a sound bite. But it is one sound bite you can start using immediately that will save you time, money and frustration in the long run. 🐔

The wonderful, wacky world of online social networking

I've been actively engaged in a number of social networking websites. Why? The answer is simple. It's the new way to meet, connect and reconnect with people, and in the process, discover new opportunities. Most of all, it's fun; there's always the unexpected surprise. On Facebook, a good friend I grew up and went through high school with reconnected with me. We hadn't seen each other since we went off to college. After connecting, he called me and we spoke for more than an hour about old times and our lives over the past 30 years.

Lately on Facebook, there's been an explosion of new groups for just about everything you can image. Individuals, businesses, and organizations set up groups. Group organizers send invitations to join to their Facebook friends – and ask friends to invite their friends.

Before you know it, the viral nature of the Internet takes over, giving groups the potential to expand rapidly. Group members can post comments or questions and even invite members to special online functions like Webinars, teleconferences or actual events at the company's physical location. It's all pretty amazing.

I pay a lot of attention to LinkedIn because it's a social networking site for business professionals – and it's all business. After giving it some effort and joining some open networker groups, I now have about 9,250 networks and 19,286,489+ contacts. I've connected with leaders from all over the world in every kind of industry imaginable. I've been invited to do Podcasts and seminars; people buy my book and share their comments.

- **Find networks that match your interests:** You must invest the time in social networking to reap the rewards. Do your research. Facebook is very social and just a great place to meet people and stay in touch. LinkedIn is where you'll find professionals. Speakersite.com is where speakers network and share.

- **You need to work at it:** All social network sites allow you to build your personal profile so others can learn about you, your interests and your expertise. Invest the time to build your profile and add content such as your bio, professional recommendations of your work, photos and videos. It's easy to identify serious social networkers because their profile pages are rich with information.

- **Sharing is where it's at:** Joining a social network and building lots of contacts only to "sell" them something is a big no-no. The opportunities come from interacting with your contacts and participating in groups. Ask a legitimate question on a group discussion, and you'll get plenty of answers. Answer questions to help others, and in the process you'll be demonstrating your expertise. That's when someone may ask you about your services or products. Share. Be respectful. Participate.

You must invest the time
in social networking
to reap the rewards.

Lastly, there's the amazing world of Twitter where devotees regularly answer the simple question, "What are you doing now?" You're limited to 140 characters so you've got to keep your answers short. I followed Lance Armstrong for a bit on Twitter and quickly learned just how tenacious and disciplined he is. Lance posted tweets all day long – after training, during a race, when he dropped his kids off for soccer, when he was with Bill Clinton in New York. Twitter is truly a social networking phenomenon.

So, expand your horizons and embrace the world of social networking. While you're at it, you can follow me at http://twitter.com/nducoff.

Every system has an 'On/Off' switch

I hate when stuff doesn't work. When I open my computer, I expect it to work; I need it to work. When I get into my car, I expect it to start; I need it to start. If you think about all the machines and other gizmos we depend on, every one has an "On/Off" switch. Flip the switch to "On," and we expect them to perform as designed.

In business, we design systems to produce specific, predictable and consistent outcomes. If you want your business to deliver world-class customer service, you need a system capable of producing that outcome. If you want to create predictable profits, you need a system capable of producing that outcome. Simply put, the systems we depend on have "On/Off" switches, too.

While giving a speech to a group of quality managers, I asked how important systems are to achieving consistent quality. After getting a collective "duh, of course!" response, I asked for the one common flaw that exists in the execution of all their quality systems. The unanimous answer was "leadership accountability." It doesn't matter how perfectly designed a system is, when you turn a system on, it doesn't mean it will stay on. Leadership with inconsistent accountability is a recipe for compromise. A compromised system will deliver something less than expected.

- **Implementing a new system is a long-term project – not a short-term task:** Systems are typically implemented with some degree of fanfare. Equate it to leaders shining a spotlight on the new system so everyone sees and pays attention to it. The switch is turned "On." Once the spotlight moves on, attention shifts. The switch is turned "Off." The process of locking in new systems, individually and in teams, is about changing behaviors – and changing behaviors is always a long-term project. Therefore, the implementation plan must include accountability checkpoints that extend months – even years – beyond the launch date.

- **Define outcomes and expectations:** Launching a new system with a "do-it-this-way" attitude is command and control. The switch is flipped to "On" without those carrying out the system knowing the "why." It's like telling your team to run a race faster without knowing where the finish line is. Complacency and indifference will eventually flip the switch to "Off." The best systems are built on a foundation of vision, clarity and understanding.

- **Systems must adapt or be replaced:** While some systems may endure a lifetime, most require modification and upgrading to remain functional and adapt to changing conditions. Some need to be replaced entirely. When the variance between the desired outcome and actual results moves in the wrong direction, it should trigger an assessment of the system. No system is sacred or above scrutiny. If it's turned "Off," turn it "On." If it's broken, fix it. If it just can't do the job, replace it.

- **System hang time is a leadership discipline:** Great companies are accountable to their systems. But accountability begins at the top. Leaders decide where to set the company's accountability bar. No-compromise leaders set the bar high for all to see and strive for. Excellence is embedded into the foundation of their company cultures. Lowering the bar is not an option. When leaders set the bar too low, their systems become fair game for compromise and routinely switch themselves to "Off." Where is your accountability bar set?

The best systems are built
on a foundation of
vision, clarity and understanding.

Take an inventory of your systems to see which ones are turned "On" and which are turned "Off." Every viable system found in the "Off" position should be viewed as a leak in the hull of your company ship. A company with too many leaks can sink just as fast as a ship.

Stuck in the vortex of 'low-level interference'

It's just lying in wait to suck you in and pull you away from the leadership work that makes great business achievements happen. And when it does get you, you'll be oblivious to the fact that you've been sucked into the vortex of "low-level interference." You'll be working full out all day like a superhero slaying dragons. You might feel as though you're in your performance zone.

Does this scenario sound familiar? You arrive at work ready and determined to dig into your project or task list. You're ready to take that first sip of your morning cup of coffee. A member of your leadership team charges up to you with a frazzled look on her face and says, "Our supply order didn't arrive yesterday and we're slammed with work today. Without those supplies, we're going to have a ton of upset customers. What are we going to do?"

You take a deep breath, take that sip of your coffee while it's still hot, and start making calls to find out where the shipment is and how to get your hands on it – fast. You just used up two precious hours.

OK, let's make this simple. You begin your day at your computer to dig through the ton of e-mails that piled up while you slept. You're an expert at identifying and deleting junk. You respond to a few of the more important ones. You're about halfway through your e-mails when your eye is attracted to a subject line.

You click on the e-mail. It intrigues you. You click on the link to the company's website where you blow 20 minutes checking it out only to conclude that you're not interested. I bet you find a few more enticing e-mails to check out. (Wow, I just did!) Without a disciplined approach to managing e-mail, you'll be repeatedly sucked into the vortex of "low-level interference."

I use the term "low-level interference" to describe all the stuff that comes at you throughout the day – every day. "Low-level interference" is on a mission to distract you, derail you, and sap your energy and time. When you finally snap out of the vortex, you realize that you accomplished nothing more than putting out fires and charging aimlessly down rabbit trails. You experience lots of action – but have little to show for it.

- **Have a daily plan:** Starting your day without a plan or task list leaves you fully exposed to "low-level interference." You're winging it and allowing your day to unfold without you at the controls. It takes just two to five minutes to organize your day. I live by my computer calendar that's synced to my iPhone. I'm lost without it.

- **Speaking of smart phones:** Chances are you have some kind of smart phone within reach at all times. (You know, that gizmo you're checking every 20 seconds to see if you have a new text message or e-mail.) Smart phones are powerful tools that can either keep you organized and on task – or suck you in the vortex of "low-level interference." I set an alarm for every appointment and "to do" in my calendar. I block time for projects – which is the equivalent of making an appointment with myself. Whenever I hear the beep beep or buzzing, it saves me from "low-level interference."

Avoiding "low-level interference" **takes personal discipline** to remain focused on your priorities.

- **Monkeys on your back:** Every time an employee comes to you with "low-level interference" stuff for you to fix – and you take the bait – you're enabling them to put their monkeys on your back. If you're not careful, you'll quickly find yourself covered with monkeys. No-compromise leaders know that taking other people's monkeys (stuff they can easily take care of if they apply themselves) is just enabling them to bring you more monkeys. Help team members to be accountable for their own monkeys and you'll be keeping "low-level interference" at bay.

- **It just takes discipline:** Avoiding "low-level interference" takes personal discipline to remain focused on your priorities. Yes, there will be times when you must deal with "low-level interference," but the key is to deal with it expeditiously and get yourself back on task. It can be as easy as asking an employee, "How can we take care of this?" Listen, then say, "That sounds like a plan. Let's get that done and get back to me later today with an update." As for the "low-level interference" you bring on yourself, learn to recognize the signs that you're off task and get back in the game.

Low-level interference is on a mission to distract you, derail you, and **sap your energy and time.**

"Low-level interference" comes at you all day, every day. It slows progress and feeds frustration as it pushes what you're capable of accomplishing just beyond your reach. The more time you spend on high-value projects, the closer you get to achieving your full potential.

Half full? Half empty?
Does it matter?

'Pay' attention

If you know anything about Strategies, you know that I'm the team-based pay (TBP) guy. Yup, I've been teaching and coaching TBP for more than 35 years. And in those 35 years, TBP has always inspired lively debate between commission diehards and TBP believers.

For the record, TBP is simply a pay system that rewards overall performance, not just sales. It provides hourly pay to reward individual overall performance in conjunction with a team bonus.

Team bonus is used to inspire and reward team performance for achieving service and retail goals as well as other key growth drivers. Everyone on the team shares in the bonus including front desk, call-center and administrative staff. More than anything, TBP creates the foundation for owners and managers to build world-class, high-performing and seriously accountable business cultures. If you want team, pay team.

Everyone is responsible. Everyone pushes in the same direction without the inherent individualistic tendencies associated with commission. Team service and client sharing thrive on TBP. Client retention, productivity, pre-booking, working within time standards and skill development become the steppingstones to pay advancement.

Retail sales thrive because it's more about adhering to a system than relying on a commission to inspire sales. Most of all, TBP gives owners the highest degree of control over the single highest cost of doing business – payroll.

Here are just some of the myths surrounding Team-Based Pay:

- **MYTH:** They'll quit if I convert to TBP.
  FACT: When TBP conversion procedures are adhered to, few (if any) employees quit. There's no reason for them to quit when integrity and trust are honored.

- **MYTH:** They won't be motivated without commission.
  FACT: How many commission employees are unproductive, disengaged or cutting back hours? On TBP, systems drive productivity.

- **MYTH:** I can't afford a fixed payroll.
  FACT: If your service payroll is higher than 30% – 35% of total revenues, you can't afford not to change. Product cost deductions and service charges are inadequate and create more trust issues than they're worth.

- **MYTH:** My top producers will leave.
  FACT: Your top producers are maxed out already. TBP provides an opportunity for continued income growth beyond commission.

- **MYTH:** I tried TBP and it didn't work.
  FACT: If all you changed was the pay, you didn't implement the entire TBP system. Commission is easy. TBP takes work and no-compromise leadership.

If you want team, pay team.

Team-based pay works. It creates amazing team cultures. It's driven by systems. It controls payroll costs and allows owners to direct pay to those who earn it in all that they do, not just for the sales they generate. ✌

Employees as partners:
Be careful what you wish for

Small-business entrepreneurs possess the vision, passion and drive to risk it all to achieve their dreams. No obstacle is too big to overcome when you're just starting out. Then, a few years down the road, the day-to-day reality of leading a successful business sets in. The lucky ones realize where their business skills fall short and hire the talent to fill those gaps. They also deal with the inevitable stress and strain of employee turnover. When turnover occurs in a key position, it can be especially frustrating and disruptive to the flow of the business.

One strategy that a growing number of small-business owners are exploring to secure leadership talent and to address the defection of key employees is to offer stock ownership in their companies. Speaking from personal experience, any form of stock distribution, through gifting, employee purchase or earned through good old sweat equity, must be clearly and objectively thought out.

Make no mistake; there are infinitely more pitfalls than benefits to making employees partners in your company. Often, the desired outcome of attracting and retaining the best talent through stock ownership doesn't work. There is a very narrow margin for error; unpleasant and challenging situations can materialize.

- **Stock doesn't make employees think like an owner:** Leaders and the cultures they create is what instill an ownership mentality in employees. Stock or "owning a piece of the business" will never transform an employee into the ideal team member. Stock ownership doesn't ensure that an employee will work harder or put in more hours. Great leaders create great employees – not stock ownership.

- **Stock ownership doesn't ensure key employees will stay:** If employees are unhappy or find a better opportunity, they will eventually leave. Would you even want a disgruntled employee to stay in your business?

Stock or not, if they're not pulling their weight, they shouldn't be on your team.

- **When an employee with stock leaves:** Making employees stockholders is a lot like getting married. It's easy to do but can become an ugly mess if you need to get out of it. Unless a sharp attorney builds in some provision for a buy-out on termination, an employee can quit or be fired and still retain his or her stock in your company, including the right to review the company's financial reports. A "buy/sell agreement" is a non-negotiable in any stock sharing transaction.

- **Minority stock ownership isn't that glamorous:** Essentially, stock ownership allows an employee to share in the profits of the company in an amount equal to the percentage they own. That's pretty much it. Minority stockholders have no voting rights or control over how the company is run. And how the company is run and how finances are managed directly relates to how much profit there is to share.

There are infinitely **more pitfalls than benefits** to making employees partners in your company.

Employee stock distribution is not a cure for retention problems nor is it a guarantee that thinking and behavior will change. However, used strategically and under the strict guidance of sound legal advice, employee stock ownership can work beautifully and effectively. 🐓

When long-time top performers drop

It's a reality that every leader must face. Top performers are those exceptional employees who get the work done. They're self-starters. They're loyal. They're mentors and role models for their teammates. They have stood by you in the both the good times and bad. Simply put, trust and appreciation flow both ways. But time, business evolution, the economy, and shifts in personal behaviors and priorities, bring leaders face to face with the toughest of business dilemmas: what to do when top performers begin to drop?

A dilemma is a situation where the possible solutions are undesirable and challenging. Long-time top performers were a joy during their quest to reach the top. They established new performance benchmarks for others to strive for. They brought consistency and predictability to the company. In the process, top performers become top income earners.

The dilemma for leaders is what to do when the performance of top performers drops and/or the company can no longer afford or sustain their high incomes. Like it or not, you need to find a solution. Avoiding or procrastinating can and will jeopardize the financial integrity of the entire company.

- **Respect time and contribution:** Long-time top performers deserve consideration for their loyalty and contribution. However, time served and contribution does not earn top performers a lifetime "get out of jail free" card. Be respectful, but still hold top performers accountable.

- **Performance is masking other serious issues:** When a top performer is doing his or her "thing," it can mask other problem performance and behavior issues. It's easy for leaders to turn a blind eye to obvious problems when they're getting the numbers they need. But when attitude, deadlines, attendance and other essential culture elements are being compromised, the company is paying a price. Such situations signal that long overdue conversations need to take place – and take place quickly.

- **Time to level the playing field:** Allowing double standards to infect your company culture is pure compromise. Entitlement behavior is toxic. Every employee can see it and knows that their leaders are allowing it to occur. If you choose not to level the playing field, stop complaining about the drama and resentment in your culture.

- **Get out of hostage mode:** Too many leaders allow themselves to get stuck in hostage mode out of fear that a top performer will quit. Here's your wake-up call: No top performer is worth keeping just because they do big numbers. Drama, attitude, resistance to change, entitlement, "all about me" anti-teamwork behavior, and all that other stuff is never worth the price your culture pays. Snap out of it! It's your thinking that's holding you hostage.

- **Pay is out of alignment:** How do you cut the pay of a top performer that gave his all for the company? This is one of the toughest decisions to make. It begins with a one-on-one to totally and completely address the good, the bad, the ugly and what needs to change. Clarify your expectations, a mutually agreed upon game and a timeline. The one non-negotiable is that pay will be reduced if change does not occur.

- **The "protect our paychecks" option:** Financial reality and the economy have a way of bringing out the no-compromise leader in people. If your company's financial reality is screaming at you to make tough decisions, you must engage. It's agonizing to let people go because you must cut payroll. It's agonizing to cut a top performer who fell out of top performer mode. You are the leader. These decisions are yours. Accountability is tough.

- **The "career opportunity" option:** If you tried coaching, serious conversations, consequences, begging and pleading, and you still can't get a top performer back on top, it's time to give that top performer a career opportunity to work elsewhere. They are sapping your energy and resources. 🐓

Performance systems: They only work if everyone plays

Performance systems exist for one purpose: to create consistent and predictable outcomes. Even the most basic of systems, such as how to answer the company phone, communicates volumes about a company's collective ability to execute tasks. And the more systematized a company is, the more efficiently and smoothly it operates. But the mere existence of systems does not ensure that the desired results will occur. Systems need to be "turned on." This requires communication, training, inspection, fine-tuning and accountability. And it is in this "turning on" phase where systems are often compromised.

The challenge of implementing systems is getting everyone to play. Just as every business culture has its loyal players, there are team members who require additional leadership and accountability attention. This group includes employees who simply have difficulty adapting to new procedures, as well as hard-core change resistors. When it comes to systems that require behaviors to change, the success or failure of implementing those systems rests squarely on the shoulders of the leaders.

- **Systems need information flow:** Every new system is designed for a reason. Everyone needs to understand what that reason is. Otherwise, it's a case of "do this" without the knowing why. People support what they understand even if it's not a popular system but a necessary one. Always communicate the "why" before the "what."

- **Systems need sense of urgency:** I always say that urgency is the energy that drives change. What is the desired outcome? What is the deadline? How will the results be tracked? How will the company benefit? How will customers benefit? What's the training program? When is the launch? Urgency is created by the necessity to change and get better. Urgency must be present at the leadership level before it can filter into the employee ranks.

- **Systems need champions:** Champions are the ones who take on new systems and run with them. Champions are part of the urgency equation because they openly demonstrate support for new systems and build momentum. Most of all, champions mentor others therefore accelerating the implementation and fine-tuning process.

- **Systems need competency training:** Systems often fail in the early stages because the training process is poorly designed or inadequate to effectively change behaviors. Give your new systems a fighting chance by channeling the necessary time and resources to succeed.

Urgency is created
by the necessity to change and get better.

- **Systems need accountability:** Allowing any player to ignore, bypass or shortcut a system is pure compromise. It creates drama, slows progress and often creates bigger culture challenges than what the system was originally created to fix. This is leadership coaching – not confrontation. If coaching fails to engage the change resistor in the new system, you must communicate respectfully what the next steps and/or consequences will be. Under no circumstances can a change resister be allowed to compromise a system that everyone else is supporting. 🐓

Is your approach to empowerment a setup for failure?

"Empowerment" is one of those overused terms that has achieved preeminent status in the world of business jargon. Without question, every leader strives to achieve that seemingly elusive state where leadership teams and employees actually think, behave and make decisions like a business owner. So why is it that in all my years of coaching leaders and businesses, only a handful of companies can truly proclaim that they have an empowered workforce? The answer is simple and may be tough for some leaders to swallow.

FACT: Too many leaders fail to understand that empowerment is an outcome. It is not something a leader bestows upon others. Empowerment is best described as a process of preparing individuals and teams to be confident, assertive and accountable. In order for that occur, leaders must be willing to invest the time, training, mentoring and resources before relaxing and letting go of the controls. Rush or short-change the preparation process and you'll see those you empowered hesitating to take action and/or making bad decisions. Some of your more over-confident team members will even charge off into roles and decision making they are totally unprepared for.

- **Clarify your expectations:** Nothing drives drama and conflict in business more than a leader's failure to clarify expectations. If you want to achieve empowerment, individuals and teams need clarity on what the objectives are and the timelines to achieve them. Empowering others to achieve vague objectives is setting your employees up for failure.

- **Train and mentor in stages:** When you empower others, you're actually charging them to think, behave and make decisions like a business owner. Problem is, even business owners mess up royally when they're unprepared. Before giving the kids the keys to the kingdom, train and mentor them in stages. Build a strong foundation in the basics of leadership, communication, financial literacy, conflict resolution, systems design and, most of all, what accountability looks like in your company. Once a strong foundation is established, you can build on each employee's or the team's strengths.

- **Empower in stages:** Every business organization has levels of authority where decisions are made. When leaders hold tight to day-to-day decision making at all or most levels, empowerment is impossible. However, when leaders prepare and then "empower" others to make decisions and be accountable within their area or level of authority – and get out of the way – empowerment becomes the outcome.

- **Open the floodgates of information:** Empowerment thrives in organizations with rapid and concise information-flow systems. I'm not talking information overload. I'm talking about the daily flow of vital information that allows the best decisions to be made at any given time – in each level of authority. Any interference or slow down in information flow usually results in bad decisions and a degrading of urgency.

- **Empowerment done right deserves recognition:** If you truly want to become an empowered organization, you must recognize and celebrate empowerment wins. If you can't find a way to spotlight and celebrate the right behaviors, don't even think about becoming an empowered organization.

Empowerment is an outcome.

A company cannot grow if the leader is plugged into and controls every element of the organization. That's the command-and-control business model that leaves little room for empowerment. Set yourself free to focus on growth initiatives by preparing individuals and teams to make the best decisions for the company. It will reveal a whole new world of opportunity for your company – and everyone associated with it.

Let's give this recession a new name

If Las Vegas had been taking bets on how long this recession would last, any bet would have been a bad bet. We all knew we were in it long before economists made it official. In the spring of 2010, economists announced that the recession was over. Huh? Well, if the recession is over, then we really need to give this "thing" we're in a new name.

Personally, I think "Fred" has a nice ring to it. Like an unwanted houseguest, Fred showed up, moved in, and now we can't figure out how to get him out. Yup, let's just rename the recession "Fred." (I bet I could make Fred into an action figure that says stupid things. This could be huge. I could make millions off of Fred. Wanna invest?) Clearly, our buddy Fred has settled into your favorite chair, is drinking your beer and working his way through your vintage wine collection. The burning question we all keep asking is, "When and how do we get Fred to leave?"

One thing for sure, Fred's overstayed welcome has created some new realities for business leaders:

- **Too many leaks can stall or sink your business:** Leaks could be just about anything, such as problem employees, cost overruns, client-retention challenges, broken or missing systems, accountability issues and more. They're those compromises that you ignore at first, but they eventually grow into major gaping holes below your company's waterline. You must tackle problems early, or they will definitely get out of hand.

- **Adding debt is not a solution:** You cannot finance your way through or out of this recession. Even though traditional financing sources through lending institutions have become next to impossible to obtain, entrepreneurs still seem to find ways to add debt. More than anything, piling on credit card debt will throw you into the fiery pits of financial hell. Trying to gain ground while dragging debt from yesterday's expenses will make any progress difficult at best. Stop spending.

- **The recovery will not be a return to what was:** Yes, we are in the throes of a major economic reset. When the economy waves goodbye to Fred, business behaviors, thinking and practices will be different. Both consumers and businesses will make buying decisions more cautiously than ever.

- **Price will challenge traditional customer loyalties:** Everyone is looking for a better deal – that means you, your team and every aspect of your business will fight harder for customer loyalty. Leaders must totally overhaul their "value-added" strategies to prevent "price predators" from stealing market share. Once your strategy shifts to competing on price, it's hard to escape from it.

- **If it feels as though you're working harder than ever, you're right:** Not only has Fred taught us to do more with less – he taught us that deals take more work to close, attracting new customers takes more energy and creativity, and that there are never enough hours in the day to get all the work done. Until further notice, working smarter and harder is the rule.

"Fred" has a nice ring to it.

- **Your business model needs to adapt at a faster pace:** The moment you think you have your business model just right – start questioning it and exploring what needs to change. At no other time in my years as a business leader have I seen business models go obsolete so fast. I'd rather be on the offensive and keep my business model ahead of the curve than play defense and catch up. If you and your company are resistant to change today, your business model is already behind the curve.

Fred will eventually move on. What he'll leave behind is a new set of strict no-compromise rules and disciplines for business success. Learn them well – and learn them fast. 🐓

Business survival in crazy times

There is only one word that accurately describes doing business in today's economy: unforgiving. The competition is relentless. Customers are more cautious, calculating and demanding with their buying decisions and their expectations. But it's not the threats from the world around you that could throw your business into a tailspin; it's what's occurring inside your business that makes you vulnerable.

The key to surviving and thriving in these crazy times begins with leadership and its determination to win the business game.

1. **No hesitation, procrastination, blame or excuses:** Ignore even the smallest problem today and a bigger problem will be waiting for you tomorrow.

2. **All lift – no drag:** A business cannot maintain or gain momentum if it's dragging anchors. Profit-draining projects, departments, services, products, locations and any other business function or entity that's not performing needs to get fixed or cut. Get unproductive employees into the game, or cut them loose. You get the picture.

3. **Live by your cash-flow plan:** If you don't have a cash-flow plan, you and your company are flying financially blind. If you have one, it only works if you're accountable to it.

4. **Have the tough conversations:** Every leader has a number of conversations that have been waiting too long to happen. Employees need to know where they stand, even if it's not what they want to hear. If you've been fighting harder to protect an employee's paycheck then the employee, it's time for you and the employee to make some decisions.

5. **Innovate to grow:** A crisis always seems to inspire innovative thinking. But why wait until there's a crisis? Get your team's creative juices flowing now. Create an environment and culture of innovation by creating

think tanks and special project teams. The next new opportunity for your company is waiting to be discovered. Go for it.

6. **Inspire a sense of urgency:** Urgency is the energy that drives business growth. Urgency pushes leaders, employees and companies out of their lethargic comfort zones. Huddles, scoreboards, deadlines, goals, rewards and celebrations are all tools to keep urgency levels high. Yes, urgency comes from leadership. It rarely happens on its own.

7. **Finish what you start:** "We've tried that before and it didn't work." If this quote describes your company's track record for getting things done, compromise is alive and well in your culture. This is all about accountability – and it begins with you.

8. **Keep commitments:** Broken promises and commitments compromise trust and contaminate business cultures. If you say you're going to do something, do it.

9. **Find that 20% growth:** I absolutely believe that every company has 20% more growth waiting to happen – if it goes after it. There are new customers and opportunities for growth everywhere. There's only one question: Are you willing to do whatever it takes to go for it? Get out of your comfort zone. Make those extra 10 sales calls. It may even be as basic as holding everyone accountable to existing systems and procedures.

The next new opportunity for your company is **waiting to be discovered.**

10. **Lead with passion:** If you truly believe in your company, its people and its mission, then let it show. Leaders who live in fear or feel like a hostage in their own company allowed their passion to fade away. If necessary, fall in love with your company again. Get fired up about the opportunities and rewards that await you. Let your passion out and your people will follow you. 🐓

An Entrepreneurial Manifesto: Part 1

I have been an entrepreneur for almost my entire working life. I have experienced the elation of success and the crush of failure. My chosen path as a speaker, writer and consultant keeps me hardwired into the thinking and behavior of entrepreneurial leaders.

Just as I marvel at their innovations and tenacity, I cringe at their self-inflicted damage when their thinking and behavior runs amuck. Through it all, there is one sacred and magnificent absolute that every entrepreneur owns: They are in control of their destinies.

A recent segment on the evening news focused on the dismal unemployment statistics. It detailed how tens of thousands of government employees are experiencing the unthinkable – they're getting laid off. A fireman who thought he had a career for life is now figuring out how to care for his family. At a center for writing resumes and honing interview skills, a dozen white-collar executives and engineers – all in their mid-fifties – are trying to comprehend the reality that no one wants to hire people their age. NASA workers celebrated the final flight of the Space Shuttle, knowing that pink slips would follow the Shuttle's return to earth.

Entrepreneurs will never lose their jobs because of downsizing or budget cuts. We lose our jobs when we mess up, make bad decisions or fail to take decisive action. And if our companies tank, we invent new ones. How long entrepreneurs remain unemployed has more to do with how long it takes them to get up, dust themselves off, and get back in the game.

- **Don't squander it:** You have the power to change and influence lives and the world around you in the most positive way. You create opportunities and careers for others who buy into your dream and choose to join your quest. It is your entrepreneurial duty to push the envelope of possibilities. It is your leadership duty to inspire and bring out the best in others, so they can realize their full potential in concert with you. When you get complacent, you squander a world of opportunity.

- **Stop whining:** Starting and leading a company is seriously tough work. You will encounter major roadblocks. You will have to work harder than ever before. Those you trust the most will compromise that trust. You will have to forfeit your paycheck to protect the paychecks of others. But you control your destiny. You can do something right now to change your situation and banish the things you don't like about your company. Stop whining and do something about it. Whining is a waste of time.

- **Never get too full of yourself:** You don't know it all. You don't have an endless bank account of good luck that ensures every risk will be a winner. People will not continue to follow you when it becomes all about you and not about the dream they signed on for. So when you feel that head of yours starting to swell, stick a pin in it. And when those around you are trying to tell you to replant yourself on solid ground, listen. If you don't, you will be contaminating your own culture.

When you get complacent, you squander a world of opportunity.

- **It's OK to question yourself:** There is nothing weak or wrong when you question your abilities as a leader. Leadership is one tough job full of hard decisions, raise-your-blood-pressure conversations and trying to stretch one dollar into two. At times the stress can seem unbearable. You cannot be master of all things. You will drive yourself nuts trying to be the perfect leader. When you question your abilities, you're simply doing a self-evaluation. And all evaluations should conclude with next steps. Do you need coaching to help you deal with a situation? Do you need to hire someone with specific expertise to complement you where you are weak? You control your own destiny. You can innovate new possibilities. You can be human. It's OK.

- **Allow others into your world:** The best entrepreneurs surround themselves with talent. More importantly, they allow the right people with the right talent to join them behind their curtain. You cannot do it all, and you cannot do it alone. Your inner circle makes you stronger and wiser. Your inner circle will be honest with you and tell you the truth when you need to hear it most. That is, if you can put your shields down and listen. Going it alone is like trying to be the Wizard of Oz, who's really just a little guy hiding behind the curtain pretending to be big and powerful.

- **Honor, respect and integrity:** Your dream is powerful and enticing enough for others to want to take the journey with you. They are not just employees; they are followers of your dream. They not only believe in you, they trust you. Sure, you have all the risk and have everything you own on the line. You must honor and respect their loyalty while practicing the highest levels of integrity.

- **It's only about the dream:** Your team may respect and be loyal to you, but it's the dream – your dream – they hitched their wagon to. Over the years, I've been hired to figure out why a company went stagnant only to find that it's the dream that went dark. It became all about the numbers, hitting goal and sticking to the budget. All that numbers, and financial and performance reports do is measure progress to making the dream a reality. I don't work hard for the money. I work hard for the dream I have for building an extraordinary coaching and training company. If I do that, the money will come. All the reports do is chart progress – and my effectiveness as a leader. It's about the dream. You still remember how to dream about extraordinary dreams, don't you? Close your eyes. Without constraint, allow your wildest dreams of success for your company to manifest in your mind. Is the impossible really so impossible?

- **Honor your accomplishments:** Hey, you got a lot right. You can sap and waste your energy on all the stuff that isn't right with your company. Snap out of it. You're an entrepreneur who controls your own destiny. You built a company and hit some bumps in the road or a major roadblock. You can stop and complain about it, or you can plot a new course. The only reason for a company to fail is when the leader disengages and accepts defeat. It's hard to talk an entrepreneur off the ledge who lost faith in his or her ability to create the right outcomes. Honor the good stuff you've done. Celebrate it. Magnify what's great about your company. Polish up that dream until it's shining bright for all to see – even you.

It's the dream – your dream – employees hitched their wagon to.

There is no way I could allow myself, an entrepreneur, to be a unemployment statistic. I am in control of my own destiny. I've seen the fiery pits of hell and the view from the top of the mountain of success. I respect that hanging at the top of that mountain is a long-term commitment that many are not willing to make. It is about acknowledging and honoring that you are in control of your destiny. And in the process, you are responsible for the destiny of those who believe in and follow your dream.

Never compromise your dream. Be the no-compromise leader your dream demands. Just go for it. What's the worst than can happen? What's the best that can happen?

And there is my entrepreneurial manifesto. Go for it. 🐔

An Entrepreneurial Manifesto: Part 2

Entrepreneurs control their own destinies. But too often, their thinking and behavior get in the way. They hold back when charging forward is the best and logical option. They fail to manage the inevitable stress that accompanies business ownership, which leads to self-doubt and feelings of isolation. They get too engrossed in emotional attachments that cloud their thinking and ability to make and execute the best decisions for the company – their dream.

In order to truly control your own destiny, here are my no-compromise additions to my entrepreneurial manifesto:

- **Change first:** As a leadership and business consultant, I'm hired by a leader to fix problems. That usually translates into "fixing" everybody else to achieve the results and outcomes the leader wants. After assessing all of the intricacies of the situation to see where the breadcrumbs lead, the source of the problem almost always is the leader who hired me. And getting leaders to change their thinking and behavior is about the toughest part of the work I do. Even when leaders acknowledge their contribution to the problem, getting them to accept and embrace change is like a persistent game of arm wrestling. To live the entrepreneurial manifesto, leaders must not only embrace change, they must model it every day.

- **You are not your company:** The company is your dream – your creation. You invest money, blood, sweat and tears into your company. But, the reality is that it is your company – your company is not you. Consider this: If entrepreneurs strike out on their own to control their own destiny, why do they get stuck in their own companies? By stuck I'm referring to being consumed with work 24/7. I'm referring to the micro-management where your leadership tentacles are plugged into every facet of the company. I'm talking about the inability to let go of the controls and lead. Lastly, I'm talking about how owners who become "their company" compromise its value when it comes time to sell. Without the founder, the company is lost. You are not your company.

- **Don't let your emotions rule:** You cannot lead without making unpopular decisions. You cannot please everyone. You cannot compromise the integrity and security of the company to avoid damaging personal relationships. You cannot accept mediocrity while fighting to take your company to the next level. You chose to be an entrepreneur. You chose to be a leader. Do it with integrity, respect, compassion and purpose. Making the right decisions for your company is hard when you allow your emotions to rule your thinking and behavior.

- **Do what others will not:** You want to be the best? You want to blow away your competition? You want fiercely loyal customers? Then you must do what others will not. It's one thing to set high standards of performance, it's another to achieve and consistently maintain and refine high standards. Getting to the next level means climbing a steeper grade. Too many stop when the going gets tough. That's accepting "average." Being an entrepreneur means pushing the innovation envelope in all that you do.

You cannot accept mediocrity
while fighting to take
your company to the next level.

- **Push forward when you think you can't:** Those who know me know my passion for road biking. I did a 68-mile fund-raising ride with my friend Mark through the magnificent scenery of Connecticut's countryside. As the day wore on, the heat climbed well into the 90s. About a third of the way into the ride, we entered a stretch of relentless hills, many with steep grades that turn your legs into rubber and sap your energy. After an hour or so of this torture and the sweltering heat, I was close to throwing in the towel. I wanted to stop in the worst way. I kept pushing forward. It was hard. Really hard. As we headed south toward Long Island Sound, the terrain leveled out. I got my second wind and finished the ride. Mark and I did our "high fives." It's the same in business. Pushing forward when you think you can't almost always takes you to a better place. When you quit, you never know the taste of victory.

- **Keep it glowing:** Your dream of creating and building a company must be kept glowing as brightly as a silver trophy. It's why you became an entrepreneur. It's why you risked everything. It's why employees were captivated enough to follow you, some for many years. It's why customers buy from you. There will be those times when the going gets tough and the obstacles appear insurmountable. It's in these times when you need to keep your dream glowing bright. Dreams can become dusty, tarnished and dented. It's your dream that keeps you and your company pressing forward. It's always about the dream.

You are an entrepreneur. You control your destiny. Seize the opportunities. Break through the barriers and roadblocks. You know they're not really big enough to stop you. It's what entrepreneurs do.

When you quit,
you never know
the taste of victory.

Stop. Breathe. Appreciate.

Take time to reflect and recharge.

Get your whole organization to join the No-Compromise revolution!

Ready for an energizing, witty, insightful, no-punches-pulled speaker?

Make Neil Ducoff your choice for your next conference,
sales meeting, corporate retreat or annual meeting.
He can easily customize his presentation to meet your specific needs.
He'll rally the troops and get everyone – at every level – on the path
to achieving no-compromise excellence.

For more information on Neil's keynotes, leadership coaching
and workshops (public and private) – call 800.417.4848
or e-mail Neil directly at neil@strategies.com.

"As the premier resort in the Sacramento Region, Arden Hills Resort Club & Spa's management and staff have all benefited from Neil Ducoff's systems, books and business philosophies. Ducoff's unique no-compromise leadership approach consistently enables our management team to work through interpersonal roadblocks and difficult personnel decisions, and create departmental systems to maximize productivity and collaboration. His books and business values are paramount for any business leader looking to achieve success within their organization."

Scott Sharrow, general manager
Arden Hills Resort Club & Spa
Sacramento, California